MW00605438

Wicked
PRESCOTT

Wicked PRESCOTT

Parker Anderson

THE
History
PRESS

Published by The History Press
Charleston, SC
www.historypress.net

Copyright © 2016 by Parker Anderson
All rights reserved

Front cover, top right: Undated picture of Prescott resident Joseph Drew (on horse). *Sharlot Hall Museum.*

First published 2016

Manufactured in the United States

ISBN 978.1.46711.952.8

Library of Congress Control Number: 2015957666

Notice: The information in this book is true and complete to the best of our knowledge. It is offered without guarantee on the part of the author or The History Press. The author and The History Press disclaim all liability in connection with the use of this book.

All rights reserved. No part of this book may be reproduced or transmitted in any form whatsoever without prior written permission from the publisher except in the case of brief quotations embodied in critical articles and reviews.

CONTENTS

CONTENTS

ACKNOWLEDGEMENTS

A book of this kind is never possible without the kind and generous help of many individuals. Specific thanks should go to the staff of Sharlot Hall Museum Library and Archives in Prescott, Arizona, for making their holdings available to me for research; Libby Coyner of the Arizona State Library and Archives for providing me with early Arizona prison records; Julie Holst of the Yavapai Cemetery Association for information on Prescott's historic Citizens Cemetery; and David and Lois Schmittinger for proofreading and editing suggestions. And thank you to my friend David Schmittinger for his invaluable assistance and for arranging the graphics and layout for this book. I could not have completed this project without them.

INTRODUCTION

The city of Prescott, established in 1864, lies in Central Arizona in the high desert, surrounded by mountains and Ponderosa pine trees. It is a thriving metropolitan area with a population that exceeds forty thousand today (not counting the equally large separate city of Prescott Valley, nine miles east of Prescott, which was founded in 1966). The growth of Prescott has been extraordinary in recent years, with the population having quadrupled in size since 1980.

In the late nineteenth and early twentieth centuries, the chief source of Prescott's economy was mining, mostly copper. This was true of most inhabited Arizona communities in those early days. There came a time, largely by the 1950s, when the mining started to die out. Many mining towns in Arizona evaporated and became ghost towns. Prescott survived, and today its economy is based on tourism, retail and its reputation for being a beautiful city for retirement.

Prescott has always been a respectable town, but every respectable town has its, shall we say, less than stellar areas. This was true of many mining towns in America. After a long day or long week of work, miners wanted liquor and women (usually in that order). Every mining town back then had numerous saloons that were always profitable, and these towns also had so-called red-light districts, where prostitutes plied their trade in "houses of ill repute." Contrary to what is portrayed in generations of western movies, prostitutes and "shady ladies" generally did not operate out of saloons.

In Prescott, the saloons were on "Whiskey Row" along Montezuma Street, and the ladies of the evening, and their houses and cribs, were one block away on Granite Street.

Many "straight-laced" people, upon reading books like this one, are shocked to learn that so-called moral laws are a fairly recent phenomenon in the big scheme of things. Prior to the World War I era, prostitution and hard narcotics were frowned upon but were perfectly legal. Many of us have grandparents who have glowingly told us of the good old days when everyone was generally honest, no one had sex before marriage, court sentences could not be appealed and so forth. Of course, none of this is true.

Crime tended to be rampant in the less reputable sections of town, and Prescott was no different. Drunken men would kill one another over gambling disputes; men would kill women who allegedly wronged them and then often were granted leniency from the courts exclusively presided over by men. Prescott had its share of such goings-on in its early history, and this book will recount a number of stories from the wicked side of Prescott from those years. Unlike many sensational books that rely on third-hand reports and legends, I have endeavored to utilize mostly original primary sources such as newspapers, court records and other records. Much folklore exists about early Prescott. Folklore makes for great entertainment on bus tours, but serious historians will settle for nothing less than known facts.

THE U.S. GOVERNMENT
CREATES ARIZONA

In 1846, the United States went to war with Mexico over land in the belief that we were destined, as a great nation, to reach across the continent from the Atlantic Ocean to the Pacific. President James K. Polk called this Manifest Destiny.

When Mexico surrendered and signed the Treaty of Guadalupe Hidalgo on February 2, 1848, it was forced to turn over to the United States more than half of its national land, consisting of what is today Texas, New Mexico, Arizona, Nevada, the lower half of California and areas of Colorado and Wyoming. It was the single largest land acquisition in American history. Today, resentment still lingers among the people of Mexico over what they see as a major land grab; children are taught in school history classes the story of how the gringos stole their land. Remember this the next time you see news reports about Mexican demonstrators crying, "*Reconquista!*"

Having acquired all of this new land, the United States did not seem to have an organized plan for how to explore, map or settle it, and so it let much of it lay there. The California gold rush of the 1850s brought many settlers to that area, and Texas was slowly being colonized. The land in between—Arizona and New Mexico—remained inhabited mostly by various Indian tribes, including the hostile Apaches.

In 1853, a group of businessmen from the southern states, with strong connections in Washington, came up with a business scheme to build a railroad that would stretch from the Mississippi River to the gold rush fields of California. Believing that such a route could not be constructed over the Rocky Mountains, these businessmen looked farther south to find an appropriate route. They decided on a pass just below the Gila River. However, that land was still owned by Mexico and was not part of the Treaty of Guadalupe Hidalgo. So these businessmen called in some markers in Washington, and predictably enough, the U.S. government quickly dispatched General James Gadsden, an army man about whom little is known, to Mexico to negotiate the purchase of more land.

Following the Treaty of Guadalupe Hidalgo, General Santa Ana had become the total dictator of Mexico. Perhaps because Mexico knew it could not withstand another war with America or perhaps because Santa Ana was thoroughly corrupt, he agreed to sell to America all of the land between the Gila River and the Rio Grande. The deal was signed and sealed on December 30, 1853, as the Gadsden Purchase, and among today's residents of Mexico, it is as reviled as the Treaty of Guadalupe Hidalgo. Supposedly, Santa Ana pocketed the money personally instead of turning it over to the Mexican treasury. Ironically, after all of this effort, the railroad was never built.

THE FATHER OF ARIZONA

Charles Debrille Poston was born on April 20, 1825, in Elizabethtown, Kentucky, the same area where Abraham Lincoln was born and raised. In fact, Poston's family and Lincoln's family were friends, a connection that would come in handy for Poston years later when he was lobbying in Washington for Arizona to be granted territorial status.

Orphaned at the age of twelve, Poston was apprenticed to Samuel Haycraft, a law clerk, and eventually married Haycraft's daughter Margaret. But like so many, Poston heard the call of "Go West, Young Man," and he set out for California. His wife stayed behind with her father while Poston was away trying to make good. They remained married, although Poston and Margaret seldom saw each other during their entire marriage, and had one daughter, Sarah Lee Poston.

Arriving in San Francisco at the height of the gold rush, Poston obtained a job as a clerk at the San Francisco Customs House. This was actually more of a private club where Bay Area bankers sat around, sipping alcohol and talking about how important they were. Poston was gifted with a silver tongue and, seeking both adventures and money, made several of the bankers an offer to explore the newly acquired Gadsden Purchase, to map and assess the area for possible mining and development. Remarkably, the bankers accepted. With their financing, Poston and Herman Ehrenberg (a mining engineer) recruited some men and set sail for the Mexican seaport of Guaymas, from where they planned to move upward into the Gadsden Purchase.

The Poston/Ehrenberg expedition accomplished its mission of mapping and exploring the Gadsden Purchase. After this, the men sailed down the Gila River for Fort Yuma, where Poston became acquainted with the military post's commander, General Samuel P. Heintzelman, and formed a lasting friendship.

Charles Poston then traveled to Washington to report his findings on the Gadsden Purchase to U.S. government officials, who weren't particularly interested. After all, they had only bought the land so that rich businessmen could build a railroad through it. However, Poston saw mining opportunities in the land, and with his silver tongue and powers of persuasion, he secured financing from New York brokers for a mining company to be set up in the Gadsden Purchase. The Sonora Exploring and Mining Company was founded in 1859. Samuel Heintzelman became the president of the company, and Poston was the on-site managing supervisor.

The company set up shop in the abandoned Mexican Presidio of Tubac, where later Poston also created Arizona's first newspaper, the *Arizonian*. The mining operations produced around $3,000 per day until the start of the Civil War. When Union troops were withdrawn from Arizona to fight against the South, Poston and his crew were left alone and unprotected from the local Indian tribes. The Apache Indians saw this as an opportunity to drive the white man from the area and laid siege to Tubac. Poston and his crew fled and somehow made it safely to California.

Returning to Washington, Poston and Heintzelman began lobbying Congress and President Lincoln to officially proclaim Arizona an

An undated portrait of Charles Debrille Poston, probably taken in the 1870s. *Public domain image, U.S. National Archives and Records Administration.*

American territory, which would open the area up to having a local government, and mining and settling of the territory could commence. Convinced, Congress passed the Arizona Organic Act in February 1864, and it was signed into law by President Lincoln. The first Arizona territorial government officials were then appointed. John Noble Goodwin from Maine was appointed governor after Ohio congressman John Addison Gurley, who was the first choice, died before taking office. Richard McCormick of New York was appointed secretary of the territory. In a gesture of ingratitude to the man who had lobbied so hard for Arizona, Poston was ignominiously appointed superintendent of Indian affairs in Arizona, a minor position and an omen of his fate to come.

When the first governor's party arrived in Arizona in 1864, they set up shop along the Granite Creek in central Arizona. This is where they, and other settlers, formed the town they named Prescott, in honor of the Boston-based historian William Hickling Prescott. Richard McCormick, the secretary of the territory, started Prescott's first newspaper, the *Arizona Miner*, that same year.

Still ambitious, Charles Poston ran for election in 1864 for the coveted position as the first territorial delegate to the U.S. House of Representatives from Arizona. He won, to the dismay of the new Arizona government officials, each of whom wanted the honor for themselves. As delegate to Congress, Poston introduced various bills to establish Indian reservations in Arizona.

Up for reelection in 1865, Poston was soundly defeated by Governor John Noble Goodwin, who clearly wanted to leave the wild frontier of Arizona. Poston did not take his election loss well and charged that he was the victim of voter fraud. He penned and distributed a "broadside" to try and rouse public anger, charging that McCormick's Prescott newspaper, the *Arizona Miner*, had falsely printed in the August 9, 1865 edition that Poston had withdrawn and was endorsing Goodwin. Poston further stated that McCormick had personally assured him that Goodwin was supporting him for reelection; therefore, he was unaware of what was happening while he was in Washington.

Was this true? Most issues of the *Arizona Miner* from 1865 have not survived, including the August 9 edition, so we cannot verify Poston's claim today. Furthermore, contemporary Arizona historians are favorably inclined toward Goodwin and McCormick; therefore, they usually scoff at the Poston charges.

At any rate, seeing the chance to finish off Poston's political career for good, the Arizona territorial legislature, now led by Richard McCormick, who became governor after John Goodwin departed for Washington, passed an official resolution condemning Poston for his allegations.

This did, indeed, put a nail in the political coffin of Charles Debrille Poston. He never again held public office and held only a variety of menial jobs, some of which allowed him to travel overseas. He wrote several books on his travels and occasional columns for newspapers. While visiting a tribe of Parsees in India, Poston became very interested in their religion of Zoroastrianism and eventually converted to it. Returning to Arizona, he purchased a mountain outside Florence and attempted to raise money to build a fire temple to Zoroaster. Needless to say, in the late nineteenth century, this endeavor caused him to be roundly laughed at and denigrated.

By 1897, many years after his downfall, Charles Poston was living in poverty in a slum section of Phoenix and was discovered there by Whitelaw Reid, editor of the *New York Tribune* newspaper (and former vice-presidential candidate in 1892).

Outraged that the man who had done so much for the creation and settlement of Arizona had ended up like this, Reid wrote a newspaper article about Poston's plight. Embarrassed, the Arizona territorial legislature voted in 1899 to give Poston a meager pension of twenty-five dollars per month, which was increased to thirty-five dollars in 1901. On June 24, 1902, Charles Debrille Poston died in poverty in Phoenix and was buried in a pauper's grave.

By 1925, due to the efforts of Arizona historians such as the famed Sharlot Mabridth Hall, Poston's work had been rediscovered. In an attempt to atone for their forefathers' shameful treatment of him, the State of Arizona

The original burial site of Charles D. Poston—a pauper's grave in an unidentified Phoenix cemetery. *Sharlot Hall Museum.*

Years later, Poston's remains were moved to this tomb on a hill not far from Globe, the very hill where he had once hoped to build a Zoroastrian fire temple. Historian David Schmittinger stands beside the tomb. *Lois Schmittinger.*

exhumed Poston and reburied him on the mountain where he had once hoped to build the fire temple, under a pyramid signifying his Zoroastrian faith. Arizona governor George W.P. Hunt presided over the official ceremony.

Today, the legacy of Charles Debrille Poston remains controversial among Arizona historians. He has been dubbed the "Father of Arizona" by those who believe the territory might not have been created as early as it was without his lobbying and exploring. On the other side, there are historians who consider Poston to be a vastly overrated figure who richly deserved the scorn that was heaped on him during his lifetime. I have actually read an article in a reputable historical journal where the author claims that, in Poston's writings on early Arizona, he was off by a few weeks on the date he arrived in Guaymas, and consequently, this calls into question the credibility of anything he ever said or did.

Wicked politics indeed.

THE TERRITORY OF ARIZONA CREATES PRESCOTT

When President Lincoln signed the Organic Act on February 20, 1863, officially creating the territory of Arizona, it was required that he appoint a set of officials and send them west to set up a new territorial government for Arizona. Initially, he appointed Ohio congressman John Addison Gurley to be governor, but Mr. Gurley unexpectedly died before the group departed. On the recommendation of Richard McCormick, Lincoln appointed former Maine congressman John Noble Goodwin to the post. McCormick became secretary of the Arizona territory.

The first governor's party traveled overland by coach—a long journey. They were informally expected to set up the new Arizona capital at Tucson, an old Mexican pueblo, which was the only sizable town in the new territory. After crossing the Great Plains into Arizona in December 1863, Governor Goodwin was informed by General James H. Carleton that Tucson was a wild place and believed to be a hotbed of Confederate sympathizers (the Civil War was still going on at this time).

They stopped at Fort Whipple, then located at Del Rio Springs (north of what is today Chino Valley), where the governor's party got their bearings and decide what to do. After much scouting and debating, they moved farther south of Fort Whipple and stopped by the banks of the Granite Creek. This area was inhabited by only a few stray miners and settlers, but the Arizona territorial officials decided this was the place to establish Arizona's first capital. They set up shop and christened the new town as Prescott. It was here that the first territorial legislature was elected.

Arizona's first territorial officials pose for a portrait before departing for the new frontier. *From left to right:* Henry W. Fleury, Joseph P. Allyn, Milton Duffield, Governor John N. Goodwin, Alman Gage and Richard C. McCormick, who would later become Arizona's second governor. *Sharlot Hall Museum.*

The citizens of Tucson were very angry that their town was not declared the capital of Arizona, as had been expected. They fought back, and only a scant three years later, in 1867, the legislature passed a bill formally moving the capital to Tucson. Richard McCormick, who had become governor by then, supported the measure. The territorial government packed up and headed to Tucson, with the exception of Henry W. Fleury, who held down a variety of positions in the government, including personal secretary to both Goodwin and McCormick. Astounded at the move, he stayed behind in Prescott and became one of its pioneer citizens, serving occasionally as probate judge and justice of the peace for Prescott precinct.

Ten years later, in 1877, the capital dispute came up again, resulting in the territorial legislature moving the capital *back* to Prescott. This held until 1889, when territorial governor C. Meyer Zulick and legislator John Robbins speedily pushed a bill through that moved the capital to Phoenix. Many Prescott citizens had gone on record as saying they would react with force to any attempt to move the capital out of Prescott. Therefore, the legislature passed the bill quietly, Governor Zulick signed it, and the officials quickly loaded up everything they needed onto a train and headed out for Los Angeles, where they stayed a couple of days to celebrate, and then transferred the shipment onto a train for Phoenix. The people of Prescott didn't know what happened until it was too late. They swore that if Governor Zulick ever came anywhere near Prescott, he would be murdered.

So why did the Arizona territorial legislature move the capital around so much? In retrospect, it seems absurd considering that situations like this never existed in other states or territories. In his later writings, Charles Poston claimed it was a power struggle by different areas of the territory to control who got elected as territorial delegate to the U.S. House of Representatives (a position Richard McCormick successfully attained after moving the capital to Tucson). This is as good an explanation as any for the bizarre scenario.

Conrad Meyer Zulick, the governor who oversaw the final removal of the capital to Phoenix, had not been popular because of his support for creating Indian reservations instead of simply wiping out the tribes with brute force. It got worse for him after the capital was established in Phoenix. He was turned out of office in 1889, when Benjamin Harrison became president of the United States. In those days, territorial governors were chosen by the president instead of being elected. Zulick retired to New Jersey, where he died.

Many years later, in an interview now reposited at Northern Arizona University in Flagstaff, former U.S. senator Ralph Henry Cameron of Arizona (a very controversial figure in his own right), claimed to have been the driving force behind persuading Zulick to move the capital in order to enhance property values in the Phoenix area. Cameron also claimed to have been on the trains that moved the capital to Los Angeles and then on to Phoenix. While Cameron had a penchant for overstating his involvement in various important events, there is also no evidence to disprove his involvement with the capital transfer.

Even after Arizona statehood was attained in 1912, the capital stayed in Phoenix, where it remains to this day. This is unlikely to ever change. However, with the explosive growth of the Prescott area in recent years, some Prescott citizens have made comments about possibly someday wresting the capital back from Phoenix once again. While they are no doubt joking, or at least half joking for now, many a mindset has been revealed through jests.

Prescott's First Murdered Woman

By 1870, Prescott had become a prosperous mining town. As the population increased, so did businesses and so did the crime rate. All mining towns had a section where the saloons were located. For Prescott, this came to be a section of Montezuma Street, which was unofficially and unceremoniously referred to as Whiskey Row. There were reportedly as many as forty saloons on Whiskey Row at one point. Miners would come here after hard work and/or getting paid, and they would blow off steam. Many frequented the brothels that had opened as well, as prostitution was legal then.

One night in mid-September 1870, Prescott's postmaster (identified only as Barnard in news accounts) was getting ready for bed when he heard a woman screaming a few houses down on Cortez Street. Rushing to assist her, Barnard burst into the house and found a prostitute (or rather, a "lady of easy virtue," as the *Arizona Miner* newspaper called her) named Jenny Shultz lying on the floor, with a man sitting on the bed holding a gun on her.

Postmaster Barnard ordered the man to put down the gun and come out. Instead, the man turned to Shultz and demanded ten dollars from her. When she refused, Barnard and the man began arguing, and then abruptly, the man turned to the woman and fired his gun, killing her.

Before the postmaster could stop him, the man ran from the house. Barnard went for Sheriff John Taylor, and they and some other men went looking for the murderer. They found him a few blocks away, chatting with two other men. The posse drew their guns, and the murderer surrendered.

The killer was identified as William Gertrude. He was found guilty and sentenced to ten years in prison (the sentence was light undoubtedly because his victim was just a "lady of easy virtue"). Since the Arizona Territorial Prison had not yet been built at Yuma, prisoners from around the territory were sent to the regular jailhouse in Yuma. The territorial prison would later be built partly due to jail overcrowding in Yuma. William Gertrude was sent to Yuma to serve his sentence.

On December 21, 1872, two years later, the *Miner* newspaper reported, with disgust, that Gertrude had been released from prison. This report was apparently erroneous, as Gertrude broke out of jail on March 24, 1873, but was apprehended the same night. He was fined $400 for the escape attempt, to be deducted at the rate of $1 per day (meaning that they tacked on four extra months to his ten-year prison sentence).

William Gertrude escaped from prison once again in November 1873, and this time he made it to Coyote Wells, California, in San Diego County. A Yavapai County deputy (from Prescott) tracked him down there and apprehended the fugitive murderer. Gertrude reportedly told the deputy that he was out of his jurisdiction, but the law enforcement official was armed with a double-barreled shotgun and Gertrude went quietly.

The fate of William Gertrude is not conclusively known. A much later newspaper account referencing the case stated that he was eventually freed from prison early due to a legal technicality. As for his victim, Jenny Shultz was the first woman to be murdered in Prescott, but not the last.

In fact, scarcely two months after Jenny Shultz was murdered, another courtesan from Prescott's red-light district, Nellie Stackhouse, was found strangled in her bed. The twenty-five-year-old prostitute was discovered by a friend (undoubtedly another prostitute), and Yavapai County authorities persuaded territorial governor Anson P.K. Safford to issue a $500 reward for the unknown murderer.

It was all for naught. Prescott authorities came to believe Nellie Stackhouse was murdered by a local physician, Dr. W.C. Soule, but he had made his escape and was never apprehended.

The First Hanging—
Fact and Folklore

It has not been studied prolifically by historians, but in the American Southwest, Mexicans lived under deplorable conditions and were largely viewed with animosity by the white population. It is difficult to study Mexican history from this period in America because births generally were not recorded, deaths were reported in the newspapers usually only in the cases of accidents or murders and other news references to Mexicans generally contained only crime news, much of which was probably exaggerated due to the attitudes of the era.

In one of Arizona's beleaguered Mexican settlements, just outside Camp Verde, violence erupted at the wedding of Santino Morales in April 1875. One of Morales's guests, Gregorio Eredia, became very intoxicated and threw a large stone at a guest, Antonio Aldecor, knocking him unconscious. Three men, identified as Manuel Abiles, "Cross-Eyed Jesus" Eredia (no relation to the perpetrator) and a white man, William Malone, chased Gregorio Eredia from the house.

The following day, the groom, Santino Morales, discovered the body of Gregorio Eredia in a wash, his head smashed with a spade. Yavapai County sheriff Ed Bowers was notified, and after interviewing all of the wedding guests, he arrested Abiles, Malone and Jesus Eredia. They were brought to Prescott, where all three were indicted for murder by a grand jury that consisted of such noted Yavapai County pioneers as Levi Bashford, Charles Genung and W.M. Fain.

When their trials came up, Jesus Eredia was acquitted of all charges, a remarkable event considering the racial attitudes of the day. William Malone was freed after his jury became hopelessly deadlocked. This left Manuel Abiles to face the wrath of the law alone. He was convicted of killing Gregorio Eredia and sentenced to death.

Surprisingly, for this period, a number of citizens petitioned the territorial governor, asking for clemency for Abiles. Yavapai County was still in its infancy, and perhaps the people of Prescott were a bit unnerved at the thought of their very first hanging. The governor denied the petition, the execution plans went forward and the scaffold was built.

On August 6, 1875, only four months after the murder, Manuel Abiles stated before his execution that he was indeed

An undated portrait believed to be of Manuel Abiles, the first murderer to be legally hanged in Prescott in 1875. *Sharlot Hall Museum.*

present at the murder of Gregorio Eredia but insisted that it was William Malone who delivered the fatal blow. Yavapai County sheriff Ed Bowers pulled the trap switch, and Manuel Abiles swung into eternity.

Over two years later, the November 23, 1877 edition of the *Miner* reported that three prisoners lodged in jail in Prescott, identified as Thomas Lyons, J.A. Lewis and William Jennings, were complaining that they were being visited by ghosts in their cell. The *Miner* rather jocularly speculated that it might be Abiles's ghost, perhaps giving a tour of the jail to some other spirits.

The story of Prescott's first legal hanging is fairly cut and dried, based on original newspaper accounts and William Malone's surviving court records. However, this has not stopped more contemporary folklorists from putting their own spin on the story. Sometime in the 1930s, Charles M. Clark, of the Arizona Pioneers Association, wrote a lengthy, completely different and very erroneous account of the hanging. Clark contended that Abiles was walking along, minding his own business, when he suddenly found a corpse by the side of the road. Almost immediately, a group of white men rode up and accused him of the murder. Abiles was then quickly taken to Prescott, tried, convicted and hanged. To his version of the story, Clark added a lengthy quote, complete with quotation marks, of Abiles tearfully professing his innocence from the gallows—even though Clark was not there in attendance to witness it. Author Clark then finished it up by adding that, decades later, an unidentified old man confessed to the murder from his deathbed, proving that Prescott had hanged an innocent man. Malone and Jesus Eredia are not even mentioned in this version.

It is impossible to know what Charles M. Clark hoped to accomplish with this folderol. His story is provably false in every detail, but it was taken seriously in the 1930s and has been repeated verbatim numerous times down to this day. Even some reputable historians have been taken in by this version of events. When writing about history, it is very easy to assume that the researchers who came before you got it right. This is not always the case. Contrary to folklore, Manuel Abiles was indeed guilty of at least being an accessory to murder and possibly the murder itself. Very detailed court papers and news accounts back this up; it is too detailed to be a fabrication.

In most later accounts, the murderer's name is usually spelled Aviles instead of Abiles. But whether or not he delivered the fatal blow, his was Yavapai County's first legal hanging but not the last. Ten more people went to the gallows between 1875 and 1925.

Shootout with Virgil Earp

The Earp brothers—Wyatt, Virgil, Morgan and Warren—are arguably the most legendary figures of the American Southwest, rivaling even Jesse James and Billy the Kid. There has been endless debate over their lives in terms of whether they were great heroes or little better than the "bad guys" they fought, particularly Wyatt Earp himself.

The Earps and their wives arrived in Prescott at various times in the 1870s, along with Wyatt's friend Doc Holliday. Virgil Earp had spent the most time in Prescott, arriving sometime in 1876 and holding down a variety of jobs, including night watchman and constable. He also operated a sawmill, believed (though not conclusively proven) to have been located at the base of Thumb Butte, the large mountain on the west side of Prescott overlooking the town. All of the Earps were drinkers and gamblers, so there is little doubt they spent much time on Whiskey Row.

There was trouble on Whiskey Row on the night of October 18, 1877. William Henry Harrison McCall, a Union Civil War general who, after the conflict, retired to Prescott, was playing pool in Jackson & Tompkins' Saloon when he was accosted for no real reason by two drunken men. One of them, Robert Tullos, proceeded to insult McCall with foul language, while the other man, known only as Wilson with an alias of Vaughn, held a gun on him. Perhaps the assailants were Confederate sympathizers—the Southwest was full of them after the war—and perhaps they knew McCall's background. Or perhaps it was just the alcohol. At any rate, after the men had their fun, they apparently left the saloon.

McCall believed he recognized Wilson/Vaughn as a murderer who had not been apprehended and ran out to secure a warrant for the arrest of the two drunken belligerents. Prescott constable Frank Murray was ordered to apprehend Tullos and Wilson/Vaughn and located them a few saloons down the street, where one of them had just tried to shoot a dog. When Constable Murray attempted to arrest them, they drew their guns and ordered him to leave. Then the miscreants mounted their own horses and galloped down Montezuma Street, firing their guns indiscriminately to ward off any pursuers.

Constable Murray found Yavapai County sheriff Ed Bowers nearby with U.S. marshal W.W. Standefer and Virgil Earp. Explaining the trouble, all of the men took off in different directions to try to surround Tullos and Vaughn. The law officers caught up with the gunmen farther down the banks of the Granite Creek—the fact that they had not ridden farther and faster away from downtown can only be attributed to their drunken state. Murray, Bowers, Standefer and Virgil Earp surrounded them from different directions and ordered the men to surrender. Instead of doing so, Tullos and Vaughn started shooting. The lawmen returned fire, killing the miscreants. Robert Tullos succumbed to eight bullet wounds, while Wilson/Vaughn caught a bullet to his head.

A coroner's inquest was held, presided over by local physician Dr. Warren E. Day. It concluded that the shooting of the men was justified by the officers in the proper discharge of their duty. Two years later, Virgil Earp, his brother Wyatt, Doc Holliday and their wives left Prescott for Tombstone, Arizona, and infamy, with the 1881 Gunfight at the O.K. Corral. Virgil would be on the receiving end of an assassination attempt in retaliation for that legendary incident. His arm was paralyzed for the rest of his life from this.

The saturation of Earp folklore in later years has embellished the Granite Creek firefight considerably and given more credit to Virgil Earp than perhaps was due. While he certainly behaved heroically, he performed his duty in direct cooperation with the other involved lawmen.

In 1895, Virgil Earp returned to Prescott, where he started mining. He was caught in a cave-in while working his claim in the Grizzly Mine on November 7, 1896, and suffered major broken bones. Two months later, he was still on crutches, but he eventually recovered sufficiently to take a few law enforcement positions. In November 1898, near election day, John Burns, the Republican candidate for sheriff of Yavapai County, swore out a warrant for the arrest of James and Claud Thompson, the editors of the *Jerome Reporter* newspaper over in the town of Jerome, for libel against him.

Virgil was appointed a temporary constable to serve the warrant and bring the newspapers editors in. He did so, and after posting bail, the Thompson brothers had Virgil Earp arrested for false imprisonment. This case seems to have been ultimately dismissed.

Virgil Earp and his wife, Allie, ranched near the town of Kirkland, Arizona, for a number of years after. In 1900, he briefly ran for sheriff of Yavapai County but then withdrew his candidacy for unknown reasons. Virgil and Allie later moved to Goldfield, Nevada, where he died in 1905. He is buried in Portland, Oregon.

The Skeleton on the Courthouse Plaza

The story of Prescott's second legal execution did not originate in or near Prescott but at a U.S. Army fort near Fort Mojave in Mohave County, two hundred miles away. There, on January 10, 1876, trouble apparently broke out between a group of soldiers on leave. In the wilderness far from the fort, Richard L. Lawler, a twenty-year army veteran from Oswego, New York, was beaten to death with large rocks and his body dragged for one hundred yards and dumped into the river. However, his body washed ashore on a sandbar downstream, where it was discovered.

Shortly afterward, three other soldiers from Fort Mojave were arrested for the crime—James Malone, Leopold Eith and James Henry. Henry never stood trial for the murder, and it is unclear why. Perhaps he agreed to testify against the other two in exchange for leniency. At any rate, the prisoners were turned over to the United States federal court system for justice—it is also unclear why this decision was made instead of court-martialing them. The accused murderers were taken to Mineral Park, Arizona, and arraigned.

Malone and Eith (Henry had been dropped from the case by then) were taken to Prescott, in Yavapai County, to stand trial for the murder of Richard Lawler in United States District Court in July 1877, over one year after the crime had been committed. Both were found guilty of murder in the first degree and sentenced to hang, by Judge Charles A. Tweed, despite the fact that even the newspapers agreed that the evidence against the men was totally circumstantial—there was simply no hard evidence of their guilt.

In sentencing Leopold Eith to hang, Judge Tweed dramatically intoned:

> *It very rarely occurs that in a case where the proof is wholly circumstantial the guilt is so conclusively proved as in your case. Not one incident alone, but another and another and another pointed directly at and connected you with the crime committed on that night on the tenth of January. The story of that night's crime was written in blood upon your own cast-off and concealed apparel, upon the spot where your victim was slain and on the stones and sand over the long way where the body was dragged to the banks of the river, almost as distinctly and clearly as it was told by your confederate, Malone, the day after the deed was done.*

Judge Tweed set the date for the double hanging for August 24, 1877, but this was delayed by appeals. Around August 30, 1877, a higher court commuted the sentence of Leopold Eith to life in prison and ordered that he be sent to San Quentin Prison in California. Some sympathetic citizens, perhaps other soldiers, sent a petition to president of the United States Rutherford Hayes for similar clemency for James Malone, but the chief executive refused to get involved.

The date for the execution of James Malone was reset for March 15, 1878, in the jail yard at 2:00 p.m. The same scaffold that Manuel Abiles had been hanged on three years earlier was used. U.S. marshal W.W. Standefer escorted Malone to the gallows, accompanied by several clergymen and Yavapai County sheriff Ed Bowers, who was required to pull the switch. Instead of speaking, Malone asked Reverend D.B. Wright to read aloud a written statement he had prepared. In it, Malone defiantly denied his guilt and asserted that the witnesses in his trial committed perjury. He further claimed the crime had been committed by James Henry and another soldier named Wilcox and that he could have proven all of this except for the incompetent lawyers who represented him at his trial.

Before Marshal W.W. Standefer placed the hood over his head, Malone asked to shake hands with several soldiers from Fort Mojave, whom he saw in the audience of over two hundred. These soldiers were allowed to walk up onto the scaffold and shake hands with Malone. The doomed man then asked for a drink and said to Sheriff Bowers, "Goodbye, Bowers. Since I can do no good in this world, maybe I can in another." Those were his last words.

At about 2:15 p.m., Sheriff Bowers pulled the lever and sprung the trap, and Malone was hanged. Two doctors, Dr. Ainsworth and Dr. Goodfellow,

The hanging of James Malone in the jail yard in Prescott in 1878. He is standing on the same gallows used to execute Manuel Abiles three years earlier. *Sharlot Hall Museum.*

monitored his pulse, which was dutifully recorded in the *Miner* newspaper: two to three minutes, slight struggle and effort at respiration; five and a half to six minutes, pulse 124; seven minutes, pulse lost at the wrist, but heart still beating; nine minutes, heart ceased beating; and his body was cut down at twenty minutes. The *Miner*, printing details no newspaper would add today, also revealed that Malone had a mother and brother living at 123 East Eleventh Street in New York City. Malone also asked that his body be donated to an unidentified medical school, and this was done.

As for Leopold Eith, despite the order to transfer him to San Quentin, he remained in the jail in Prescott for the next two years because the U.S. government never sent the funds for his transport. This prompted the Yavapai County district attorney, other officials and even Arizona territorial governor John Charles Fremont to petition the U.S. government to pardon Eith. There seems to be no solid surviving evidence of the outcome, but circumstantial evidence would indicate that he received a pardon and was freed.

James Malone was the second of the eleven murderers to be hanged in Prescott between 1875 and 1925. There is a strange denouement to his story. The March 24, 1882 edition of the *Miner* newspaper reported that Malone's skeleton had been stolen from the unidentified medical school, apparently by a prankster who then deposited it beside the well on the Courthouse Plaza in Prescott. This time, Prescott authorities decided to bury him, and while the records of Citizens Cemetery do not list him as a burial, it is almost certain this was where James Malone was buried, in one of the many graves that are today unidentified.

The Bloodiest Day in Court

It is a matter of some dispute as to when and where Charles Washington Beach was born. His son Louis would say in later years that his father was born in Montreal in 1833. But Charles Beach's listing in the 1880 census states that he was forty-one years old and born in Connecticut, which would put his birth year at 1840. Some then-contemporary newspaper accounts refer to Beach as having been a native of Connecticut.

At any rate, wherever Charles Beach came from, he apparently heard the call of "Go West, Young Man!" and headed for New Mexico in 1857. The following year, he married a woman named Tiburchina Mascaranas (her nickname was Hazel), who came from a prominent Albuquerque family. She bore him three children, a daughter Josephine (who was killed in a train wreck at the age of about three or four) and sons Louis and Robert.

Around 1864, Beach abandoned his wife and son Robert in New Mexico. Apparently kidnapping his son Louis, he headed for the newly formed Arizona territory and settled in the new capital of Prescott. There he started a freighting business that ran loads between Prescott and other towns and cities in the Arizona territory. The following year, he took his son Louis to the home of his half sister in Placerville, California, and simply left him there.

In 1870, Beach sold his freight business in Prescott and moved to the town of Wickenburg, where he began a new freighting operation. The following year, he married again, his second wife being a Wickenburg girl named Cora Kelsey, who seems to have kept her maiden name afterward—virtually unheard of in those days. According to accounts available at Sharlot Hall

This is the only known portrait of Charles Washington Beach, the Prescott newspaper publisher, rancher and businessman. His life was extremely controversial, though he had many friends. *Sharlot Hall Museum.*

Museum in Prescott today, Cora bore him six more children. No one has ever found a record of a divorce proceeding between him and his first wife, Tiburchina.

After marrying Cora Kelsey, Beach purchased a ranch near what is now Kirkland and continued his freighting operations. As his business was earning him a very good living, he was appointed postmaster at the post office in Kirkland in 1873. Life was good for Charles Washington Beach, a man who had abandoned his first family and was possibly a bigamist as well.

In 1876, Charles Beach purchased the *Arizona Miner* newspaper in Prescott, at that time the only paper emanating from the area. This gave him a tremendous amount of influence, both in politics and business. He was now a very important man in the Prescott region.

Troubles began for Beach in 1878, when he apparently objected to a neighboring rancher, Patrick McAteer, using water from Kirkland Creek (which Beach claimed total ownership of) to supply his ranch and cattle. Beach sued under his wife's name (for some reason), and the case was known as *Kelsey vs. McAteer.* At that time, Judge Charles Silent in Prescott ruled that McAteer was legally allowed to water his cattle within reason from the creek. But Beach and his wife were not satisfied and appealed. The case dragged on for years.

The case came to a head on December 1, 1883, in the Yavapai County Courthouse, where an appeal was being heard by Chief Justice C.G.W. French of the Arizona Territorial Supreme Court. There were conflicting accounts, to be sure, but trouble started when Yavapai County district attorney Charles Rush (representing McAteer) and Clark Churchill (attorney for Beach and his wife) started insulting each other in court. At one point, Churchill reportedly called Rush a liar and threw an inkstand (which probably weighed three or four pounds in those days) at him. A brawl broke out in court between the two attorneys, and Beach and James More (a friend of Beach from Kirkland) ran to Churchill's assistance and started beating up on District Attorney Rush. John C. Herndon, Rush's law partner, jumped into the fray to assist Rush. Patrick McAteer, who had been the defendant in Beach's lawsuits, drew a knife and jumped into the action, slashing More's left arm (later folklore that More's arm was severed completely is almost certainly not true).

At this point, Charles Beach drew his gun and shot McAteer in the back. The gunshot seems to have stopped the fracas, and there were injuries to be treated from the brawl. The case of *Kelsey vs. McAteer* was postponed until the next court term, although with the defendant in the suit dead, there wasn't much more that could be done. Prescott was shocked by the events—contrary to our views of "frontier days," incidents like this were not as common in those days as is widely believed.

Patrick McAteer lay unconscious for several weeks, eventually succumbing to his gunshot wound on January 21, 1884. Charles Beach was not arrested, the authorities deciding that he acted in self-defense (plus, he still carried a lot of weight in Yavapai County). In 1885, Beach successfully purchased McAteer's ranch in Kirkland, which included the entirety of Kirkland Creek. This made Charles Beach one of the largest ranchland owners in Yavapai County.

Life went on for Charles Beach, and it was rosy. Shortly before the courtroom brawl, he had sold the *Arizona Miner* newspaper to S.N. Holmes, who ironically died in a house fire soon after. He also was a big wheel in the forming of the Prescott and Arizona Central Railroad in 1886. Modern-day historians, though, have seized on an interesting tidbit from Prescott's other newspaper, the *Courier* (a rival to the *Miner* for many years), from January 1888. It states that Beach's wife Cora had given birth to a son, Byron Comstock Beach, in Los Angeles—not explained is why she was in Los Angeles. Furthermore, one of Beach's business partners was named William Henry Comstock. Very interesting, but no proof of anything untoward. Some later newspaper references to the Beaches would continue to place Cora Kelsey Beach in Los Angeles, indicating that perhaps they had indeed separated.

But Charles Beach's charmed life eventually ran out. On September 9, 1889, George Young, a rancher from Skull Valley, Arizona, sued his wife, Johanna, for divorce, claiming that she had been committing adultery with Beach and that, further, she had persuaded him to sell Beach three hundred head of cattle before he realized the inappropriate relationship she was having with Beach. In filing suit against his wife, Young also petitioned for custody of their three children.

There is no historical proof that Charles Beach was having an affair with Johanna Young, but in the end, this does not matter. George Young believed he had been cuckolded (the term used in bygone days), and unable to wait for the courts to act, Young soon decided to take matters into his own hands. On September 17, 1889, only a matter of days after filing suit against his wife, George Young (probably under the influence of alcohol) picked up his shotgun and went after Beach.

At that time, Beach was living in a boardinghouse on McCormick Street owned by Sarah Taylor, near where the former governor's mansion stood. Beach was in his room writing a letter to his wife in Los Angeles when Young found his window and shot him from outside. Several neighbors were alerted by the gunshots and ran outside. Several recognized Young as he fled up the hill toward the Masonic Cemetery. Yavapai County deputy Michael J. Hickey successfully tracked Young down in Skull Valley and arrested him for murder.

George Young was brought before Justice of the Peace Henry W. Fleury, who was to determine if enough evidence existed to hold Young in jail for the grand jury to act. W.H. McGrew acted as legal counsel for Young, while District Attorney Henry D. Ross acted for the territory. Among the witnesses who testified were neighbors Len Hale, Dr. Warren E. Day, boardinghouse owner Sarah Taylor and Prescott pioneer Samuel C. Miller, who gave friendly testimony for Young, claiming that Young had dined at his house earlier in the evening and then left, saying he was riding home for Skull Valley. Ultimately, Judge Fleury ordered George Young to be held on $500 bail in advance of the action of the grand jury. Five of Young's friends paid his bail, and he was released.

Charles Washington Beach was buried in Citizens Cemetery, but his grave no longer has a marker, although it doubtlessly once did. Ironically, Patrick McAteer is probably buried here as well, although no records survive to confirm this. There are many graves in Citizens Cemetery whose occupants are no longer known today. As for George Young, while out on bail, he borrowed $150 from his friend Samuel C. Miller and gave Miller a string of horses as collateral. In May 1890, while still awaiting trial, Young took his shotgun to Miller's house and demanded the return of his horses without repaying Miller the money. Another man was present at this altercation, which probably prevented Young from actually killing Miller.

George Young went on trial for murdering Charles Beach in November 1890. The jury found him guilty but strongly recommended leniency for Young because (of course) he had been wronged by a woman. The sympathetic judge complied and sentenced George Young to only three years in Yuma Territorial Prison—three years for premeditated murder.

While serving his sentence, Young's wife, Johanna, successfully sued her husband for divorce, and since he was still in prison, she was awarded custody of their three children.

After being released from prison, George moved to Mohave County in Arizona and went to work for the Tennessee Mine. In 1899, he and a mine foreman named Ferguson were giving a tour of the mine to Judge Richard E. Sloan from Prescott (Sloan would later become Arizona's last territorial governor). The three men were lowered down a deep shaft to look around. When the large bucket was positioned to draw them back up, Young got in first, but through a freak accident, the bucket became unhooked and Young fell to his death. Sloan and Ferguson climbed down a two-hundred-foot ladder to the bottom, found Young's body and assisted in conveying it back to the top. Young was taken to Phoenix and buried somewhere.

At some point, a street between McCormick and Summit Streets (near the boardinghouse where Beach was murdered) was named Beach Avenue in his honor. To the reader who may wonder why, it must be remembered that as disreputable as he may seem historically, he was a powerful and influential man who still had many friends, and was seemingly well liked, in spite of his misdeeds. Today, Beach Avenue runs only one block and is behind Sharlot Hall Museum in Prescott. Interestingly, on November 4, 1912, a worker from the Prescott city water department was digging a trench along Beach Avenue when he unearthed an old skeleton. An examination of the remains indicated the man had been dead and buried at least fifty years, dating back to the time of Prescott and Arizona's founding. Old-time residents could offer no insight, and it was speculated the dead man may have been the victim of a murder that was never discovered.

One other footnote: Tiburchina "Hazel" Mascaranas Beach, the first wife of Charles Washington Beach (from whom he may never have been officially divorced), died in Higbee, Colorado, in 1907—or was believed to have died. Embalming was not commonly done in those days except for the very rich. Hazel had asked her son Robert Beach to bury her on a hill overlooking her home (you could do this in those days), but in the end, he buried his mother in the Higbee Cemetery. Apparently feeling guilt over his failure to observe his mother's final wishes, he spent a number of sleepless nights and decided to have her exhumed and reburied on the hill per her wishes. When Hazel's coffin was dug up, she was dead all right, but there were reportedly signs that she had been buried alive: she was turned over in her casket, her face had scratches and she had pulled out some of her hair. It was one final tragic chapter in the tragic story of Charles Washington Beach.

THE MURDER OF OLD TEX

Tiptop (sometimes spelled Tip-Top) was a small mining town deep in the Southern Bradshaw Mountains in the late nineteenth century, along with similar nearby towns such as Humbug and Colombia. Today, all of these places are ghost towns. Due to the remoteness of their locations, these towns did not survive when the mining died out.

On or about April 1, 1881, a rancher named Michael P. Shores (who was nicknamed "Old Tex" by his friends) was found shot to death on a trail about seven miles from Tiptop. His body was in an advanced state of decomposition, and it was determined he had been dead for at least two weeks. As Old Tex was known to carry money and gold pieces around, it was assumed that the motive was robbery. Prescott physician Dr. Warren E. Day, accompanied by several men, traveled to Tiptop to examine the body, officially declare the cause of death and bury him. Dr. Day would later have trouble collecting a fifty-dollar fee for his services from the Yavapai County Board of Supervisors, which tried to weasel out by claiming Tiptop was in Maricopa County (which it isn't), but it ultimately paid.

In early May, the sheriff of Maricopa County arrested a man named John W. Berry on suspicion of having killed Old Tex. Berry was a former employee of the Tiptop Company, a prominent mining outfit, and had shipped out after a fight with a man named Leighton. Berry and Old Tex knew each other, and other Tiptop residents said the victim never would have traveled with strangers. Berry was first arrested in Phoenix for having stolen a saddle from a Mexican at Frog Tanks, but it was soon discovered that the bridle in

This is the mining town of Tiptop in the Southern Bradshaw Mountains of Yavapai County in the 1880s, when Michael Shores was murdered. Today, there is virtually nothing left of Tiptop except a few building foundations. *Sharlot Hall Museum.*

Berry's possession had belonged to Old Tex. This was enough to make him the number one suspect in Shores's murder. The evidence was slight against Berry, who undoubtedly claimed he had bought the bridle from Old Tex, but Yavapai County sheriff John Walker traveled to Gillette, Arizona, to pick up Berry from the Maricopa County sheriff's office and bring him to Prescott.

Berry was arraigned on June 8, 1881, on a charge of first-degree murder in the death of Michael "Old Tex" Shores. He pleaded not guilty, and the court appointed Murat Masterson to defend Berry. When Berry went to trial, one of the jurors on the case was Coles Bashford, the disgraced former governor of Wisconsin who later moved to Prescott, Arizona, to make a new name for himself as a businessman.

To no one's surprise, John Berry was found guilty of murdering Michael Shores at Tiptop and sentenced to hang. The date was set for September 23, 1881, but this was delayed because attorney Masterson filed appeals, none of which was successful. The *Miner* newspaper made note that the evidence against Berry was entirely circumstantial but felt that justice had been done.

As the day of his execution approached, Berry became increasingly nervous and refused to eat. He later relented and, as the *Miner* reported, ate one breakfast of twelve large oysters, six boiled eggs, a beefsteak, three slices of bread and a large bowl of milk.

On Friday, February 3, 1882, time ran out for John Berry. At noon, he was led to the gallows in the courtyard of the jailhouse by Sheriff John Walker and several deputies, including William J. Mulvenon, who would later become sheriff. A Catholic priest, Father Duraches, also was present. After the death warrant was read, Berry was placed on the trap by Sheriff John Walker and given a glass of whiskey. Berry declined to make a final statement and simply asked the sheriff to get it over with as quickly as possible. Those were his last words.

The black hood was placed over Berry's head, and at eight minutes past noon, Sheriff John Walker sprung the trap and John Berry plunged to his death for the murder of Michael Shores. At 12:24 p.m., he was pronounced dead, and his body was cut down and placed in a pine box. Although no records survive to show the place of burial, he was undoubtedly interred in Citizens Cemetery in one of the many graves that are now listed as "unknown." Of the eleven men legally hanged for murder in Prescott between 1875 and 1925, Berry was the third. The scaffold was not immediately taken down, for reasons we shall see in the next chapter.

GOODBYE, OLD BOY

In the early days of the Arizona territory, Coconino County had not yet been formed, and Yavapai County was therefore much larger than it is today, with its borders stretching to the Utah line. Flagstaff was a part of Yavapai County then, although the county seat was in Prescott. This story begins in Flagstaff.

On the morning of September 24, 1881, about 7:00 a.m., two armed men walked into a Flagstaff saloon owned by a proprietor named H.J. Bishop. Their names were Henry H. Hall and Robert D. McBride. Apparently they had been drinking and carousing all night, and even though it was dawn, they still weren't finished. The two drunken men demanded service from Bishop, who refused and ordered them to leave. Hall and McBride pulled their guns in a rage and opened fire on the saloon owner. Bishop managed to grab his own gun and return fire before collapsing and dying. Both Hall and McBride were hit but fled the saloon.

Angry Flagstaff citizens formed a vigilante committee to hunt down and lynch the murderers. However, by the time they got their act together, the proper authorities had already caught up with Hall and McBride. After obtaining medical help for their wounds, they were taken to Prescott, the county seat, where they would be tried.

Henry H. Hall and Robert D. McBride went on trial in Prescott on November 9, 1881, with Judge C.G.W. French presiding. For some reason, the jury found McBride guilty of only second-degree murder, and he was sentenced to ten years at Yuma Territorial Prison. He was pardoned by territorial governor Frederick A. Tritle on November 23, 1883—a scant two years into his sentence. Hall, however, was found guilty of first-degree murder and sentenced to be hanged.

The day of Hall's execution was set for February 10, 1882, exactly one week after the hanging of John Berry. Prescott authorities probably had not even taken the scaffold down yet. The day before his hanging, a reporter from the *Miner* requested an interview with Hall and found the doomed man quite talkative. Despite facing imminent death, Henry H. Hall decided to go out with a bang and told the reporter a lot of wild stories about himself that are difficult, if not impossible, to verify today. Hall claimed he was a Civil War veteran who served in the Union army and had been sent on a number of secret missions to do unsavory things that he refused to elaborate on. He also claimed to have been shot and wounded six times during the war. He also claimed to have been a deputy sheriff (he did not say where) who had once been forced to kill a man in the line of duty.

Hall told the *Miner* that he was fifty years old and a widower with a twenty-one-year-old son. As for the crime for which he was about to die, Hall denied killing Bishop and claimed it had been done by others after Bishop provoked them. He said a Flagstaff resident named Barriclow would vouch for his character.

Continuing to entertain the reporter from the *Miner*, Hall stated that he was acquainted with some cattle rustlers in Flagstaff who sported names like Blind Jim, Deadwood Charley, Hurricane Bill, Josh Lock, Chuckaluck Jimmy, Long Me, Ed Gorman, Horse Thief Bill and Three Band Jimmy. Hall should have been writing dime novels.

There were rumors that some of Hall's friends might try to storm the jail and rescue him, so Sheriff John Walker put a number of extra guards on duty. Nothing happened.

On February 10, 1881, at 11:52 a.m., Henry H. Hall was led onto the scaffold in the jail yard in Prescott by Sheriff John Walker. Before being pinioned, he knelt and prayed. Then, asked if he had any last words, he requested that the newspaper reporters be brought to the front so they could hear him, and then he spoke:

> *I wish to return thanks to my attorney, Charles B. Rush, and my heartfelt thanks to those who have ever in anywise wronged me and hope God will also forgive them. I had no ill feelings against Bishop. He was my friend, and I have been convicted through malice. I have not the language at my command with which to properly give my thanks to Mr. C.B. Rush. I*

*forgive everybody in this world and hope God will forgive us all. At best, life
is short, and it is but a little while until we all will be on the other shore.*

One reporter, identified only as "Colonel Bigelow," called out and asked
him if Henry H. Hall was his real name. Hall replied that it was not and that
he left his real name with his attorneys, who would reveal it later. Then he
said to Bigelow, "Goodbye, old boy." Those were his last words.

The black cap was pulled over Hall's head and the noose adjusted. Sheriff
John Walker sprung the trap and Hall was hanged. Two doctors, Ainsworth
and McCandless, monitored his pulse, once again dutifully reported in the
Miner: at two minutes after hanging, his pulse was at 171; at three minutes,
165; at four minutes, 158; at five minutes, 126; at six minutes, 112; at seven
minutes, 94; at eight minutes, 109; at nine minutes, 93; at ten minutes, 82;
and at eleven minutes, there was no pulse and Hall was declared dead.

Henry H. Hall was undoubtedly buried in Citizens Cemetery, although
the surviving records do not list him there. Again, there are many unknown
graves there, and Hall is surely one of them. Attorney Rush revealed
afterward that Hall stated that his real name was Hill, not Hall (one has to
wonder if he was just being snide). The doomed man had apparently also
asked Rush to tell the media that he (Hall) had killed somewhere between
fifteen and eighteen men in his life, but Hall naturally left behind no details.
Of the eleven men legally hanged in Prescott between 1875 and 1925,
Henry H. Hall was number four.

In the week following Hall's execution, the local townspeople of Prescott
apparently started debating whether Hall might have actually been forgiven
by God and gone to heaven, in view of his religious pronouncements on the
scaffold. This prompted a local clergyman, R.A. Windes, to write a letter
to the editor of the *Miner* in which he stated that God is not fooled by such
charades and went on to repeat the traditional Christian scorn of "deathbed
conversions." Windes wrote:

> *If he* [Hall] *had escaped he would have had no more faith today than
> he had the day he shot Bishop or any of the other sixteen he murdered.
> Whatever faith he had was scared into him, and was not that faith which
> worketh by love. We do not venture the assertion that no one can be forgiven
> near the hour of death, but we do venture the assertion that the instances
> are so extremely rare that it is impossible to get any veritable proof. I have
> personally witnessed many instances where parties thought they were going
> to die and professed religion while scared, but they did not die as expected. I*

know of no instance in which they did not return to their wickedness. One of the most celebrated physicians of my knowledge, being a Christian man, kept a record from his earliest to his latest practice, instances of repentance when death was expected. Out of over one hundred instances, not one was found to be genuine.

–Journal Miner, *February 17, 1882*

Windes then stated that anyone who argues the possibility that a man could be forgiven by God at the hour of his death was irresponsibly encouraging potential future murderers to commit their crimes. He concluded, "The instance of the thief on the cross has been woefully abused."

THE DILDA CASE

William H. Williscraft was a prominent Yavapai County rancher, businessman and photographer in the 1880s who owned more than one spread in the Walnut Creek area, roughly northwest of Prescott past Williamson Valley. As he could not be everywhere at once to look after his interests, he hired other men as caretakers (along with the usual ranch hands) to look after his interests. Most ranchers did that in those days—they had to.

To act as caretaker for his Walnut Creek ranch, Williscraft hired a young man with a wife and two small children who reportedly were the ages of four years and ten months old. Undoubtedly, they seemed like a nice family who could use the employment. The man was Dennis W. Dilda, who (he claimed, at least) hailed from Raccoon Mills, Georgia, which is today a ghost town no longer on the Georgia state map. Some historians have said his wife's first name was actually Georgia, but I have not been able to independently confirm this. Her father and other family lived in the Salt River Valley in Arizona (today Phoenix).

Sometime later, rancher Williscraft discovered some minor unidentified articles missing from another building on his ranch, and for reasons no longer known, deduced that his employee Dilda had stolen them. Williscraft rode to Prescott and swore out a warrant for Dilda's arrest for petty larceny. In those days, investigations by authorities were not always required for allegations of crime. If you felt you were a victim, or if you thought you had knowledge of a crime, you could go to the police and ask for a specific individual to be arrested, and it would be carried out without an investigation. In fact, in much of America, you could do this as late as the 1950s.

On December 20, 1885, the warrant for Dilda's arrest was given to Yavapai County deputy John M. Murphy, who proceeded out to Walnut Creek. On his way there, Murphy stopped and chatted with a neighboring resident, P.J. McCormick, who warned the lawman to be careful, as he believed Dilda possessed a volatile temper and was genuinely dangerous.

Arriving at Dennis W. Dilda's house on the Williscraft ranch, he was met by Mrs. Dilda, who told him her husband was not home. Disbelieving, Murphy searched the house (in those days, lawmen could do this without a search warrant), and not finding Dilda, he left and went to the neighboring Charles Behm ranch. Murphy left the Behm ranch to return to Dilda's house at eight or nine o'clock that night.

Around that time, from his own house on his ranch, Williscraft was startled by the sound of distant gunshots. He got on his horse and rode in the direction of the shots but thought he saw an armed man coming toward him in the dark and retreated. The next morning, he rode up to Dilda's stable, where he was confronted by Dilda, who was armed. At that moment, another ranch hand named Robert Ferguson appeared, and Dilda informed them both that he would kill any man who tried to arrest him. Deputy John Murphy was nowhere in sight.

Somehow, Williscraft and Ferguson escaped unharmed. Ferguson rode for Prescott, where he told Yavapai County sheriff William J. "Billy" Mulvenon that, while on the ranch, he had seen tracks that looked like a dead body had been dragged away from Dilda's house. Forming a posse, Sheriff Mulvenon arrived at Dilda's house. There, the body of Deputy Murphy was found in the cellar in a sack, and Dilda had fled, leaving his wife and children behind. Apparently, Dilda had ambushed Murphy and shot him, perhaps believing Murphy was going to arrest him for something more serious than petty theft. John M. Murphy was the first Yavapai County law enforcement officer to be killed in the line of duty.

The posse set off after Dilda and overtook him two miles beyond Ash Fork on December 23, when they apprehended him without a fight. While some posse members wanted to lynch him right then and there, Sheriff Mulvenon told them he would not stand for it, and the men backed down. They returned to Prescott and lodged the prisoner in jail. This created considerable excitement in Prescott. The Prescott newspaper *Arizona Miner* requested an interview with Dilda, but he refused.

This set off another mystery. Prior to swearing out the warrant for Dilda's arrest, Williscraft had noticed another one of his hired hands was

A portrait of members of the unofficial vigilante group the Prescott Rifles. Despite their uniforms and regalia, they were not an official military detachment. *From left to right*: George E. Ralph, Frank Meador and an unidentified man. Little is known of them. *Sharlot Hall Museum.*

missing, a man named James Jenkins, who was always called by his nickname of "General Grant." Williscraft had previously asked Dilda where Jenkins was, and Dilda responded that Jenkins was ill and had gone to Prescott to seek medical help. With Dilda now in jail charged with murder, Williscraft realized that "General Grant" Jenkins had never turned up.

Investigators returned to Dilda's house, where they found wheelbarrow tracks with two sets of footprints leading away from the house. They believed one set was light enough to be that of a woman. Following the tracks, they found a shallow grave about one hundred yards away, where the murdered James "General Grant" Jenkins had been buried. Undoubtedly, this murder had also been committed by Dennis W. Dilda, but his motive remains unknown. It may have been simple robbery, as Jenkins had been saving up money to return to his native England.

A local vigilante group, the Prescott Rifles, started talking about storming the jail and lynching Dilda after news came of the second murder, but they did not make good on their threats. The Rifles were similar to groups in other towns in the nineteenth-century Southwest, formed by disgruntled citizens who were dissatisfied with law enforcement in their towns and made it clear they were not above taking the law into their own hands (although they seldom did). Prescott had a second similar group at this time as well: the Prescott Grays. When Deputy John Murphy's body was brought back to Prescott, the Rifles took charge of it, even though nobody asked them. Murphy's funeral was held at the Prescott Rifles' personal armory, with large numbers of Yavapai County officials and citizens in attendance. Murphy was Catholic, so Father Franciscus X. Gubitosi from the Catholic Church presided over the ceremony, after which a large throng of mourners followed the funeral procession to Citizens Cemetery, where Murphy was buried with a traditional three-volley gun salute provided by the Prescott Rifles, even though they really were not military men. Six years later, on January 11, 1893, a large monument was erected over Murphy's grave, manufactured by J.W. Wilson & Co. It stands in Citizens Cemetery to this day.

Dilda's wife, Georgia, was also arrested for complicity in both murders, but the impaneled grand jury declined to indict her. Local resident Samuel Curtis Rogers and his family agreed to shelter Mrs. Dilda and her children while the court case was going on, though Mrs. Dilda and her children apparently later went to Phoenix to stay with her father, whose name was William Patterson.

Dilda sent for Prescott attorney Earl M. Sanford and asked him for legal representation, claiming he owned property near Phoenix that he would turn over as a fee. But Sanford was no fool. He checked out the claim, found it to be false and walked away from the case. Attorneys James J. Hyde and E.H. Cook were later appointed by the court to represent Dilda, although courts in those days were not required by law to do so (up until a Supreme Court ruling in 1962, many defendants in court were tried without counsel).

Dennis W. Dilda was brought before the grand jury and indicted for murder on December 30, 1885. He pleaded not guilty, and since court was already in session, his trial took place the following day, with Judge J.C.

Shields presiding. Yavapai County district attorney L.F. Eggers prosecuted the case, with his assistants John C. Herndon and Charles Rush. The trial lasted only one day, and the jury took all of five minutes to return a guilty verdict. Judge Shields then sentenced Dilda to death, fixing the date of his hanging for February 5, 1886. At that point, his court-appointed attorneys walked away. In those days, appeals were not automatic. A convicted criminal could appeal a conviction as long as he could retain attorneys to handle it. There would be no appeals for Dennis W. Dilda.

The crime so shocked the citizens of Prescott that many rumors flew about regarding exactly who Dilda was. The newspapers alleged that Dilda had previously killed a man in Texas but was acquitted, that there was a standing "Wanted Dead or Alive" reward for him in New Mexico, that his wife's brother had mysteriously disappeared in Phoenix and may have been killed by Dilda, that he shot at and missed more than one person in Phoenix and so forth. It is virtually impossible to know if any of these rumors were true. If they were, there may still be reposited records of the cases in existence, but without more details on where the alleged incidents occurred (such as *where* in Texas?), they would be very difficult to find, and as far as I know, no one has ever attempted it.

The night before Dilda's execution, a reporter from the *Arizona Miner* again tried to interview him, but aside from expressing gratitude for the good treatment he had received from the jailers, he refused to talk. He wrote a letter to his father and brothers in Georgia telling them what had happened to him. He was visited that night by the Sisters of Charity (a local Catholic group) hoping to persuade Dilda to convert to Catholicism before he died and thus save his soul. He then received Father Gubitosi to talk about it, but by morning, Dilda had changed his mind and refused to see the priest.

On February 5, 1886, Dilda was shaved, given a haircut and clothed in preparation for his execution (this sort of thing is still done today). He was given brandy and a pipe at his request and ate a large breakfast (dutifully reported by the *Arizona Miner* as consisting of breaded spring chicken, cream sauce, fried oysters, lamb chops, green peas, tenderloin steak with mushrooms, English pancakes with jelly, potatoes, bread and coffee). The meal he had ordered could have served five people, but as it was his final repast, Dilda made the most of it and had nearly finished it by the time he was led to the gallows.

Prescott photographer Erwin Baer stopped by the jail that morning and requested that Dilda pose for a photo with his wife and children. At first he objected but ultimately agreed. The photo survives and is reposited at Sharlot

Just before his execution in 1875, Dennis W. Dilda agreed to pose for a portrait with his family for photographer Erwin Baer. *Sharlot Hall Museum.*

Hall Museum in Prescott. Whoever donated it to the museum many years ago scribbled a note on the back stating that Dilda's wife was the sister of Ramsey Patterson, a well-known mountain lion hunter in Northern Arizona.

During the morning, various county officials visited Dilda, probably more out of curiosity than anything else. At 11:00 a.m., Sheriff Mulvenon read the death warrant to him, and he was led from the jail to a vehicle commandeered by—who else?—the Prescott Rifles. They took him to a scaffold somewhere in West Prescott; the exact location is unknown today. The hanging was public—contrary to what you see in old Hollywood movies, this was actually unusual. But about eight hundred Prescott citizens—a huge chunk of the town's population—turned out to witness the macabre event. However, contrary to folklore, there is no evidence that a marching band entertained at the hanging.

In those days, executions were carried out in the counties where the crimes occurred, and it was the job of the county sheriff to pull the switch that hanged the murderer. After being escorted from the Rifles' car, Dilda simply said, "Goodbye, boys." He was then led onto the scaffold and asked for one more swallow of whiskey, which was given him. He was then pinioned and hooded by Deputies Michael J. Hickey and George Burton. While Deputy James Tackett adjusted the noose, Sheriff Mulvenon pulled the switch and Dennis W. Dilda was hanged for his crimes, less than three minutes after being placed on the scaffold and only forty-seven days after murdering Deputy Murphy. One unexpected incident of note: future Yavapai County sheriff William O. "Buckey" O'Neill (a legendary figure in Prescott history) fainted at the sight of the hanging. The embarrassment over this haunted him for the rest of his life.

The official county physician, Dr. Ainsworth, assisted by a Fort Whipple doctor named Dr. Barrows, monitored Dilda's pulse while he was hanging there so they could pronounce him dead. The *Arizona Miner* actually reported the pulse rate in detail: at the end of the first minute, 63; second, 93; third, 94; fourth, 123; fifth, 145; sixth, 127; seventh, 126; eighth, 105; ninth, 91; tenth, 80; eleventh, 66; twelfth, 63; thirteenth, 53. By the fourteenth minute, there was no longer a discernible pulse, and at the fifteenth minute following the hanging, Dilda's body was cut down. He was quickly placed in a cheap coffin and driven to Citizens Cemetery, where he was buried in a cold, unmarked grave in a section known informally as the "Potter's Field," where the county buried the indigent, the poor, the unclaimed and other undesirables. Dilda's grave is ironically located in the same cemetery as that of his victim, John M. Murphy, but on opposite ends. Historically, there are many unknown graves in Citizens Cemetery, whose records and markers have not survived, and it is very likely that James "General Grant" Jenkins is buried somewhere here as well.

Of the eleven people executed in Yavapai County between 1875 and 1925, Dilda was the fifth.

As for Dilda's widow, the former Georgia Patterson, she apparently went on to marry a man named Ben Anderson in Buckeye, Arizona, on March 26, 1888, and had more children. In the 1960s, "old sage" historian Roger Anderson claimed to be her grandson from this union. The popular website www.findagrave.com claims she later married a third time, to George Hamlin, and that she died in Los Angeles on March 14, 1954. As for her two children by Dennis Dilda, little is known of them. Various later reports identify them as having been named Fern and John or Jesse.

Fifty years later, in an article for the *Prescott Courier* newspaper, old-time resident Henry Hartin claimed that photos of Dilda's hanging were reposited at Sharlot Hall

This is the grave of Yavapai County deputy John Murphy, who was gunned down by Dennis W. Dilda while trying to serve an arrest warrant on him. Ironically, both killer and victim are buried only a few yards from each other in Citizens Cemetery in Prescott. *David Schmittinger.*

Museum. If so, they must have been stolen somewhere along the line, as the museum does not have any photos of this particular execution, nor are any photos of the Dilda hanging known to exist anywhere else at this time, although photos were undoubtedly taken.

HORRIBLE THEY WERE

Mardi Gras in New Orleans has been celebrated for many, many generations, and its key appeal is that men (and in more modern times) women dress up in outrageously garish costumes during the festival and, by their own admission, act ridiculous. It seems funny to imagine such antics being a part of the nineteenth century (since a lot of people believe that era was so stoic), but it actually had been common throughout history in many parts of the world.

In San Francisco, a gentleman's club known as the Bohemian Club (also known as Bohemian Grove) was formed in the late 1800s, with part of its very private activities consisting of dressing up in nonsensical costumes and performing in annual rituals. The Bohemian Club exists to this day, and it reportedly still performs these activities. In more recent times, it has been the brunt of right-wing conspiracy theories because so many of its members have been, and still are, rich and powerful people.

But these activities took place in the large cities in nineteenth-century America. Things like this didn't happen in small burgs like Prescott, Arizona. Or did they?

In 1881, Prescott residents W.F. Holden and John F. Meador (very little is known about either man) decided to stage something memorable for Prescott's July Fourth celebrations in 1881. They and some friends formed a parade for celebration in which they named themselves "the Horribles." On July 4, 1881, at 2:00 p.m., they burst forth upon the streets of Prescott, dressed in ludicrous costumes, singing wildly off key, playing musical instruments badly (intentionally) and acting like they were on something a little stronger than alcohol. According to the *Miner* newspaper, which described the parade in depth, the head of the parade consisted of the "Horrible Fish-horn Band" followed by a man dressed as Satan. Then came a man dressed as Lady Liberty being pushed in a dump cart by another man.

On and on the parade went, with participants dressed as animals, historical figures, you name it. The *Miner* reported that it was "transcending anything in the line of burlesque display ever seen in Arizona." The Horribles then marched to the Courthouse Plaza, where they stopped, got up and read nonsensical pronouncements, like the "Declaration of Impudence," among other things.

The merriment was so original to Prescott that residents applauded the show. With this kind of reception, the Horribles decided to return the following year. In their 1882 July Fourth parade, they tried to outdo the ludicrousness of the previous year—among many other things, a man portrayed then president Chester Arthur, who was accompanied by a man dressed in stereotypical Chinese garb in a dump cart. Horrible members marched as Mephistopheles, Oscar Wilde, Uncle Sam and various Indians. At one point, a cart appeared with a flour barrel decked out like a mule head, with a body improvised out of a bird cage. As the Horribles had become popular after their debut the year before, the parade drew more respectable citizens to participate in the outrageousness—the Prescott Rifles (remember them?) joined the parade in 1882, but as if worried they could lose respect, they were only willing to go so far as to wear white pants with yellow stripes.

The Horribles continued to march in Prescott on July 4 for years to come. Somewhere along the way, a man named Joseph Dauphin took over the group and probably was the most responsible for keeping them going. But while their marches remained popular with parade-watchers, the newness wore off, and the newspapers stopped carrying detailed descriptions of what they did, often only noting their participation. When they were mentioned, Dauphin was usually mentioned as the man in charge. Very little is known about him.

Suddenly in 1891, the Horribles outdid themselves. Their July Fourth parade that year was highly praised by the *Arizona Miner* newspaper, which stated that the "Horribles eclipsed everything in this line ever attempted before in Prescott." The marchers were dressed as characters from HMS *Pinafore*, ostriches, elephants, an old woman carrying a man on her back, knights and Roman soldiers, and one man was dressed as a bottle. The public loved it.

Part of their renewed success may have been due to the Horribles having picked up a new seamstress, Zora Morgan, who worked hard for them and

These two photos from the 1880s show the outrageous costumes and regalia worn by the Horribles in their bizarre annual celebrations. Their antics made them very popular in old Prescott. *Sharlot Hall Museum.*

designed costumes that were beyond anything the group had ever dreamed of. Mrs. Morgan (who was married to a local resident named Charles Morgan) was also the first known woman to have anything to do with the Horribles, although she never marched. Societal norms in those days did not allow women to publicly appear this way, though the parades did consist of men in drag.

Buoyed by the reception, the Horribles kept Zora Morgan as their costumer, and she continued to deliver for them, with the *Arizona Miner* singling her out for praise in 1893 and 1894 for her outfits in the parades. Her abilities drew some fame; in late July 1894, a group in Flagstaff contacted her and asked to borrow fifty of her costumes.

Zora Morgan died soon after, on October 31, 1894—fittingly, Halloween. Her obituary states that her body was shipped to Cambridge, Massachusetts, for burial. At this time, no historian has successfully located her grave, and it is likely that, over the years, it became unmarked (very common in many old cemeteries). As for the Horribles, there is no record that they ever marched again after 1894. Perhaps they were unable to find a suitable replacement for Mrs. Morgan and decided it was time to pack it in.

Today, Prescott historians are fascinated by the Horribles and are frustrated that so little information about them has survived. Only a few newspaper articles and a handful of photos remain of their memory.

Annie's Fallen Angels

Even though prostitution was legal in most of America at this time, many prostitutes still lived a life of poverty. As with any other business, some days were undoubtedly slower than others. Some of them worked for "madams," women who employed ladies of the evening in much the same way a pimp does today. Like today's pimps, many madams grew considerably wealthier than the habitués who worked for them.

In Prescott, Annie Hamilton was one such madam. The 1880 census lists her as owning a large two-story house on Granite Street and lists eight prostitutes living with her. As with most denizens of the red-light district, little is known of her, although modern-day folklorists have become attracted to the story of Annie Hamilton. A common story still being told is that in 1889 she sold her big house to Prescott mayor Morris Goldwater (uncle of future U.S. senator Barry Goldwater) and moved on. But why would a man as esteemed and highly regarded as Goldwater buy property in such a seedy, disreputable neighborhood?

In actuality, Annie Hamilton had died two years earlier in her home on Granite Street. The May 11, 1887 issue of the *Arizona Miner* reported that she was unconscious and near death and that vultures had taken this opportunity to steal her valuable diamonds. A week later, the newspaper reported her death, offering few details, undoubtedly due to her profession.

In those days, when an individual died leaving no survivors, a probate judge would appoint someone to dispose of the deceased's estate and property. It remains much the same today. After the death of Annie

Hamilton, Yavapai County probate judge William O. "Buckey" O'Neill received two applications from people wanting to administer her estate. One was from ex–county coroner Patrick Ford (who had been a Civil War hero), and the other was from attorney Louis Wollenberg, who represented Annie's creditors. The madam had apparently died leaving considerable debt, including a large sum owed to a man named McNutt, a construction contractor who helped build her house.

In the end, Judge O'Neill appointed Wollenberg to dispose of Annie Hamilton's estate. Patrick Ford was later appointed to become administrator of the estate of the notorious miner and businessman Charles P. Stanton, who had been murdered several months earlier in Southern Yavapai County, leaving no survivors. Ford, along with his son Jerome, would be arrested for arson for burning down Stanton's old house.

Wollenberg wasted no time in holding an estate sale out of Annie's house on Granite Street to pacify her creditors. Her belongings were quite impressive for a bordello madam—they consisted of seven bedroom sets in black walnut and ash; seven spring hair top mattresses; one hundred pounds of feathers in pillows and bolsters; pillowcases; blankets; sheets; quilts; three parlor sets; a piano; two French plate mirrors; oil paintings; water color paintings; etchings; steel engravings; chromos in walnut and gilt frames; parlor, hall and stair carpets; cooking stoves and parlor stoves; valises; trunks; ice chests; diamonds; earrings; finger rings; breast pins; a fur cloak and cape; dresses and many other clothing items; dining room and kitchen furniture; and so on. Prescott was amazed.

The only surviving record of a purchase from Annie Hamilton's estate sale is that of Mrs. Archibald, mother of future Prescott chief of police Miles Archibald, who bought Annie's grand piano as a gift for her daughter Maggie. Legal wrangling over the two-story house continued until December 1889, when it was sold to satisfy a lien held on the house by construction man McNutt. It was torn down years later, and Annie Hamilton was forgotten. She is likely buried in Citizens Cemetery, in one of the many unmarked graves for which there are no records of who is buried in them.

Well over a century later, in 2003, Sharlot Hall Museum's Blue Rose Theater renewed historical interest in Annie Hamilton with the play *Annie's Fallen Angels*, written and directed by Jean Lippincott and produced by Blue Rose founder Jody Drake. The play, performed at the Elks Opera House in Prescott, was a speculative account of life inside Annie's house. It was well received and spurred new interest in the madam of Granite Street.

THE CLEVENGER KILLINGS

This story did not initially begin in Prescott but in the Buckskin Mountains near the Utah border, not far from Kanab. There, in January 1887, ranch hands searching for stray cattle discovered the remains of a burned campsite. To their horror, they saw that earth erosion from recent heavy rains had uncovered a human arm protruding from the ground. Digging at the site, the ranchers unearthed two badly decomposed corpses, a man and a woman with their hands and feet locked together, one of top of the other. A coroner's inquest from Kanab concluded that the two had been murdered, their heads bashed in with an axe handle.

Kanab residents came forward and identified the victims. They were Samuel and Charlotte Clevenger, who had sold their ranch at Fort Thomas, farther south in Arizona. They were headed to Washington with their adopted fourteen-year-old daughter, Jessie, and two hired hands—a white man named Frank Wilson and a black man named John A. Johnson. These two may have been hired as escorts by the Clevenger family for their long journey. As there were only two bodies, Kanab authorities placed Wilson and Johnson high on the list of suspects. There was no trace of the girl.

The discovery of the murdered couple appeared in newspapers as far away as San Francisco, but it didn't seem to be a Yavapai County issue until Sheriff William J. "Billy" Mulvenon was informed that the crime took place in Yavapai County and therefore was in his jurisdiction. Coconino County in Arizona had not yet been formed, and the borders of Yavapai County extended to the Utah line.

So perhaps grudgingly, Sheriff Mulvenon headed to Kanab, Utah, to try to strike the trail of the murderers, even though the coroner concluded that the Clevengers had likely been dead for many months before their bodies were discovered. Once there, Mulvenon received a tip that Wilson and Johnson had gone to Bullionville, Utah, and separated. When he arrived in Bullionville, residents told the sheriff that they believed that John Johnson had gone to Duckwater, Nevada. Traveling there, Mulvenon located Johnson working on a ranch and arrested him (issues of legal jurisdiction were not so rigidly enforced in those days). Johnson, hoping for a break, told the sheriff that Frank Wilson had taken the young Jessie Clevenger to Oakdale, Idaho.

Sheriff William J. "Billy" Mulvenon is seen in this undated portrait. He presided over three hangings in Prescott, the most for any Yavapai County sheriff. *Sharlot Hall Museum.*

Determined to get his man, Sheriff Mulvenon traveled to Oakdale, Idaho, and found Wilson and the girl with little difficulty. Like Johnson, Wilson undoubtedly felt he had made it far away from the legal jurisdiction of Arizona. The sheriff brought the three fugitives to Prescott, which was the county seat of Yavapai County, and lodged them in jail. The city newspapers praised Mulvenon for his tenacity in traveling all over the country to bring in the murderers. For their part, Frank Wilson and John A. Johnson were both quickly indicted for first-degree murder, while the fourteen-year-old Jessie Clevenger was indicted for being an accessory in the murder of her parents. Both Wilson and Johnson denied their guilt and blamed each other for actually committing the murders. District attorney John C. Herndon eventually dropped the charges against the girl in exchange for her testimony.

On the stand, young Jessie Clevenger told a horrible story about how on May 21, 1886 (over six months before the bodies were discovered), Johnson murdered her father while Wilson slew her mother. Following that, Wilson forced her to stay with him as his "wife" and threatened to kill her if she ever tried to escape. She repeated the story verbatim several times and could not be shaken under fierce cross-examination by defense attorneys John Howard and L.F. Eggers (who had switched sides since the Dilda case and were now working as defense attorneys).

The jury took only a few minutes to find Wilson and Johnson guilty of first-degree murder for killing Samuel and Charlotte Clevenger. Judge J.H. Wright sentenced both of them to be hanged on August 12, 1887. As with Dilda, there were no appeals.

In the course of the trial, Prescott newspapers revealed that Wilson had once previously been indicted in Pima County for horse stealing but that Samuel Clevenger had helped him out of that scrape. John Johnson was a military veteran, a former member of the Tenth (colored) Cavalry in Baltimore, Maryland.

Preparations were made for what was expected to be Prescott's first double hanging, and Sheriff Mulvenon ordered the rope that was to be used. But in the interim, Frank Wilson unexpectedly wrote out a confession to the murders in which he took full blame for killing the Clevengers and stated that Johnson had not participated in the actual murders. Prescott residents and the authorities were skeptical over the statement, but defense attorneys Howard and Eggers took it to territorial governor C. Meyer Zulick in hopes of getting Johnson's death sentence commuted.

The *Prescott Courier*, in printing Wilson's confession, reported that he had stated that Jessie Clevenger helped bury the bodies. From jail, Wilson indignantly wrote to the *Courier*:

> Ed. Courier—*Dear Sir: In your paper of 10th instant there is an article headed "Wilson's Confession." I did make a statement in which I admitted that I killed Clevenger and his wife and that I alone am responsible for the crime of which Johnson and myself are convicted, but I never said that Jessie Clevenger helped me to bury the bodies of Clevenger and his wife. I never even mentioned her name in my statement. If you will correct that mistake you will greatly oblige a murderer. Frank Wilson.*

The *Courier* printed the letter but did not fully retract its previous statement.

In talking to the press, the condemned man stated that Frank Wilson was not his real name but refused to divulge his true identity so that his family would not be disgraced. If he was telling the truth, his real name has never been discovered, and his real family, whoever they were, would have only known he was missing and never accounted for.

After the deathwatch began, members of the clergy, including Catholic priest Father Franciscus X. Gubitosi and protestant ministers W.L. Allbright, J.C. Houghton and Reverend C.C. Wright, called at the jail, but Wilson, professing no belief in God, refused to see them. Johnson, however, took solace from their visits. A Mrs. Bishop from the Holiness Mission also visited but was treated scornfully by Wilson.

On the morning of the hangings, a very pregnant Jessie Clevenger asked Sheriff Mulvenon to allow her to speak to Wilson. He agreed (this would almost certainly not be allowed today), but the conversation reportedly resulted in the girl accusing Wilson of having lied about Johnson's innocence. Wilson remained very calm all morning, smoking cigars while waiting for the time to go by. Johnson was more fearful of his impending death.

Governor Zulick came up from Phoenix to attend the executions. But at noon, the time for the hangings, Zulick handed Sheriff Mulvenon a reprieve for Johnson (no doubt the result of Wilson's written confession), giving him until September 23 to file appeals and/or obtain further evidence to clear himself. Upon hearing of this literal last-second reprieve, John A. Johnson broke down and wept.

Immediately after, Frank Wilson was taken into the gallows yard that had been built on the Courthouse Plaza for the occasion, accompanied by Sheriff Mulvenon and Deputy Michael J. Hickey. Asked for his final words, Wilson repeated that he alone had murdered the Clevengers, bid goodbye to everyone and stepped onto the death trap while the lawmen pinioned him. Sheriff Mulvenon pulled the switch, and Frank Wilson plunged to his death at 12:12 p.m. His body was then removed and taken to Citizens Cemetery for burial (it should be noted that records for the cemetery do not list him, but again, there are many unknown graves here, and Wilson is undoubtedly in one of them. Under the circumstances, he would not have been shipped anywhere else). Between 1875 and 1925, there were eleven legal hangings in Yavapai County. Frank Wilson was number six. Photos were undoubtedly taken of the hanging but are not known to have survived.

On August 30, 1887, only a couple of weeks after the hanging, fifteen-year-old Jessie Clevenger gave birth to Wilson's child, a girl. It is not known what became of them.

When John A. Johnson failed to provide further evidence of his innocence by the September 23 deadline, Governor Zulick reprieved him again until October 22, 1887. Following that, Zulick gave in to doubt and commuted

The grave of Sheriff William J. Mulvenon in Mountain View Cemetery in Prescott. *David Schmittinger.*

Johnson's sentence to life in prison. This decision, especially coming from a governor as unpopular as Zulick already was, evoked outrage from residents of Yavapai County, who did not believe Wilson's statement that Johnson was only an accessory after the fact.

John A. Johnson spent a number of years in Yuma Territorial Prison and was eventually pardoned by territorial governor John Irwin on January 15, 1897. Following his release, Johnson drifted around for a while, getting into petty scrapes with the law. At one point, many years after the Clevenger murders, he returned to Prescott for reasons unknown and was arrested for vagrancy and threatening his landlady, a Mrs. Grisalda, in April 1907. His eventual fate is not known.

In the years following the hanging of Frank Wilson, Prescott old-timers and folklorists often speculated about Wilson's confession. Some of them concluded that, while in jail awaiting execution, Wilson and Johnson played a card game of "seven up" with the loser agreeing to swear an affidavit exonerating the other. This story continues to be told in Prescott folklore, but whether it is true is one of those things that will never be known.

I Guess I Will
Go Asleep Now

As previously noted in "Goodbye, Old Boy," Coconino County had not been formed by the 1880s, and the borders of Yavapai County stretched to the Utah border. Prescott was the county seat, and people with court business had to travel a great distance from some of the outlying towns. Flagstaff was part of Yavapai County until 1891.

In the "Mexican section" of Flagstaff in 1887, a young man named Martin Duran (who claimed to be only eighteen years old) became enamored of a young woman, twenty-three-year-old Reyes Baca. The couple began cohabiting, even though they were not legally married. At some point, the relationship went sour, and the young and beautiful Reyes Baca moved out of Duran's house and moved in with another Mexican woman. Reportedly, Reyes Baca became romantically involved with another man.

This was more than Martin Duran could bear. On the night of September 18, 1887, he gathered together some of his friends, and they went to the home of the two women to serenade them. It is reasonable to assume they had been drinking. The women, who were awakened by the serenade, invited the men to come in. They sent out for beer and socialized for a while, and then Martin Duran asked Reyes Baca to come back to him. Although she was flattered by his persistence, she refused. Shortly thereafter, she turned away to adjust a lamp, at which point Duran pulled out a gun and shot Reyes Baca through the head at point-blank range. By bringing a gun, he clearly had planned to kill her if she refused to come back to him.

Duran made no attempt to flee the scene and was quickly arrested. He was taken to Prescott, where he pleaded not guilty to first-degree murder. He was tried and sentenced to be hanged, despite a vigorous defense by attorneys John Howard and L.F. Eggers. Martin Duran took the stand in his own defense and, despite his plea of not guilty, freely admitted to the murder (through a Spanish interpreter), apparently believing that his claim of having been wronged by a woman would resonate with men everywhere. It did not, although if Duran had been white, it might have. After such testimony, attorneys Howard and Eggers had very little to work with.

Judge J.H. Wright sentenced Duran to be hanged on January 20, 1888, but this was postponed until March 2 while John Howard, L.F. Eggers and other sympathetic parties, most notably Prescott's Catholic priest Father Franciscus X. Gubitosi, appealed for clemency to territorial governor C. Meyer Zulick. These efforts failed—perhaps Zulick was still feeling burned by the anger over his sparing of John A. Johnson, who was black. Father Gubitosi was particularly sympathetic to Duran's plight and stayed with Governor Zulick until after midnight the day before the execution, pleading with him to spare the young man's life or to at least delay the hanging long enough to send for a Mexican priest to officiate. Gubitosi then returned to Prescott to administer the last rites to Duran.

On the morning of March 2, 1888, Martin Duran was shaved, dressed and prepared for execution. Father Gubitosi administered last rites and absolution. Duran asked a Mexican jail trusty, Jesus Melendez, to write to his brother and tell him what happened. He also gave a fellow prisoner, Antone Romero, the address of a friend and asked him to write to him also.

Shortly before the hanging, Father Gubitosi appealed to Sheriff William J. "Billy" Mulvenon to delay the hanging for another forty minutes while he made one final appeal to Governor Zulick by telegraph. Mulvenon agreed, but this appeal failed also. The priest was so overcome and angered by the whole situation that he refused to ascend the gallows with Duran, as was usually the custom. The only plausible explanation for there being so much sympathy for Martin Duran was—you guessed it—that he was wronged by a woman.

Martin Duran feared his death greatly. He was so overcome he could barely stand or walk. At 1:30 p.m., Sheriff Mulvenon read the death warrant to Duran, translated by Jesus Melendez. The procession started to the scaffold, with the prisoner having to be assisted with walking by Sheriff Mulvenon and his deputies. At one point, Duran was reported to say, "My God, this is tough."

On the scaffold, Antone Romero read aloud from a prayer book (in the conspicuous absence of Father Gubitosi), and Martin Duran was asked if he had any final words. He made a few remarks about white man's justice, shook hands with those on the scaffold and said goodbye to his friends. He then said, "I guess I will go asleep now" as the black cap was pulled over his head. He requested that a silk handkerchief be tied around his neck to lessen the few seconds of pain he might feel while he was hanged.

At 1:37 p.m., Sheriff Mulvenon sprung the trap ("trap" was used in the old days in hangman's terms), sending the young murderer to his death. Three local doctors pronounced him dead eight minutes later, and the body was cut down and sent off for burial. There is no official surviving record of where Martin Duran is buried, but it had to be Citizens Cemetery. In fact, there are two unmarked graves that cemetery records list simply as "Hanged Mexican." If the records are correct, Martin Duran is surely one of them. The other is likely Manuel Abiles, hanged in 1875. Again, there are no known surviving photographs of the hanging, although some were surely taken.

Of the eleven legal hangings in Prescott between 1875 and 1925, Martin Duran was the seventh. He was also the only one of these eleven to be executed for killing a woman. Of these eleven hangings, three of them were presided over by Sheriff Mulvenon, the most for any Yavapai County sheriff. Mulvenon had previously sprung the trap at the hangings of Dennis W. Dilda in 1886 and Frank Wilson in 1887.

The Man Who Could Not Stay Out of Trouble

Louis C. Miller was born in Texas to a large family with many brothers and sisters. They were a railroading family, yet Miller was the only one of the male siblings who did not work on the railroad. Young Louis heard the call of law enforcement. Unfortunately, he had a fiery hot temper and extremely poor judgment, a bad combination that kept him in trouble all his life.

He arrived in Prescott sometime in the early 1890s and, in 1893, was elected constable for Prescott precinct. This was, and still is, a comparatively minor law enforcement position, consisting of serving legal papers, making minor arrests and night watchman–style duties, even though Prescott also had a night watchman. Miller's life started to deteriorate in January 1894.

At that time, Justice of the Peace Henry W. Fleury had asked Constable Miller to serve an arrest warrant on a low-life man known only as "Red" for beating up a woman (probably on Granite Street). Red, however, had already been picked up by Prescott chief of police Miles Archibald, who took the prisoner to the hospital for treatment of an unknown minor injury. Undaunted, Miller went to the hospital and took custody of Red, forcibly withdrawing him from medical treatment, and hauled him off to jail. Chief Archibald was not pleased by the constable overriding his authority.

Later that evening, the two lawmen confronted each other outside of a Whiskey Row saloon. They argued over who had proper custody of Red, and the argument ended with Constable Miller drawing his gun and shooting Chief Archibald twice.

The shooting was the talk of Prescott. The constable had shot the chief of police? Archibald (who survived but lost the use of his right arm) claimed that Miller had fired on him unprovoked. Miller, in turn, claimed that Archibald had drawn his gun on him and that he fired in self-defense. The young constable was arrested for the attempted murder of Miles Archibald. An understandably confused grand jury refused to indict him, and he was set free. Miles Archibald resigned as chief of police and went to San Francisco to seek treatment for his arm. Miller retained his job as constable.

Within weeks of the Archibald shooting, Constable Louis C. Miller was back in hot water. He responded to a disturbance on Granite Street in which a prostitute named Marie Castro was screaming at a drunken man named John Wallace to leave her house. When Miller tried to break up the trouble, a scuffle of some kind apparently ensued, and Constable Miller shot Wallace (who miraculously survived). Again, Miller claimed self-defense, alleging that Wallace had grabbed him by the throat and was choking him.

This incident resulted in a nasty war of words between Prescott's two newspapers, the *Journal Miner* and the *Prescott Courier*. The publisher of the *Courier*, Colonel Edward A. Rogers, was a friend of Miller and directed the paper to side with him, describing Wallace as "full of whiskey and in a maniacal frame of mind." The *Journal Miner* came down against Miller, depicting Wallace as a man so intoxicated he could hardly stand up, let alone attack a strong young man like Constable Miller. The two newspapers then started to publicly accuse each other of fabricating the details, facts and figures of the story. It was not Prescott journalism's finest hour.

Louis C. Miller was again arrested for attempted murder, and this time he went to trial. However, the jury believed his claims of self-defense and acquitted him. Buoyed by his victories in court, Miller announced his candidacy for sheriff of Yavapai County in the coming elections that year. Colonel Rogers and the *Prescott Courier* endorsed him, but the Yavapai County Republican Party refused to go near Miller in the wake of his notoriety, and he withdrew from the race and ran again for constable but was defeated.

This was not the end of Miller's life of trouble. We will catch up with him again later in this book.

THE BLUE DICK

As it is today, prostitution was usually a lifelong career for those who practiced it. In the red-light district of Granite Street in Prescott, one of the better known habitués was Estella Shanks, a black woman with dyed reddish hair who was known on the streets as the Blue Dick. Prescott authorities believed she had originally come from Kansas, and at the time of her death in 1909, she had been on the streets of Prescott for roughly twenty-five years.

There were not many African Americans in Prescott to begin with, so a black prostitute stood out. At first, one may wince at her crude-sounding "professional" name, but it may not have come about for the reasons one might think. There was an active mine in Yavapai County called the Blue Dick, and historians believe that Estella sometimes traveled there to service the miners.

On July 30, 1895, a Prescott man named John George Blessing swore out a warrant for the arrest of the Blue Dick, charging that she had stolen $200 from him. The circumstances of the alleged theft are unknown, but one can speculate that Blessing believed that Estella Shanks had cleaned out his billfold while he was…er…preoccupied. She was arrested and brought before Justice of the Peace Henry W. Fleury, who ordered her held for the grand jury on $500 bail. Interestingly, two men, J.F. McCoy and R.E. Conklin, came forward and paid her bail. It is not known why; perhaps they were regular customers (and therefore friends) of hers.

Estella "Blue Dick" Shanks went on trial for grand larceny on June 9, 1896. The jury acquitted her the next day. The reason for this is up for conjecture—in those days, only men could serve on juries. Perhaps the jurymen in the Blue Dick's trial thought they might be able to collect some favors from the notorious prostitute, and perhaps they did.

On July 2, 1909, Estella Shanks was found dead in her room on Granite Street. She was likely in her fifties. At the time of her death, she was sitting on the floor leaning against a wall and apparently had just gone to sleep. The *Journal Miner* newspaper, in reporting the death, erroneously listed her name as "Bella Shants" and ignorantly reported how surprising it was that the authorities found $326.25 in cash hidden in her room (a considerable amount of money in those days). But this was not really surprising—many prostitutes saved much of their money, often with the dream of someday having enough to break free of that life, although few have ever succeeded. The *Journal Miner* also noted how "peculiar" it was that the entire sum that was found was made up of $1.00 bills or silver dollars. Again, one wonders why the anonymous newspaper reporter thought that odd—$1.00 was probably Shanks's going rate, and that was a lot more money in 1909 than it is today.

The Blue Dick was buried in Citizens Cemetery but, oddly, not in the Potter's Field, where most people who were deemed disreputable were buried in those days. An unverifiable local legend contends that a wealthy friend sprung for her grave in the more respectable section of the graveyard. But Estella Shanks was not destined to rest in peace. Sometime in the 1960s, a decision was made to widen Sheldon Street in Prescott, and doing so wiped out four rows of graves in Citizens Cemetery, including that of Estella Shanks. This is sadly a common occurrence—when developers look for prime real estate, they often look at old, closed cemeteries. I am aware of at least two entire cemeteries in Arizona that were wiped out for this reason, and in Arizona and many other states, there are no laws to prevent this.

The Highway Department claimed it exhumed all of the bodies and reburied them in a mass grave at Rolling Hills Cemetery, near the Prescott Airport. But Pat Atchison, the founder of the Yavapai Cemetery Association, told me personally that she spent years trying to find the official record of the mass exhumation but had no success.

Rolling Hills Cemetery does have enough space that a large, unmarked mass grave could indeed be there, and it probably is. But at the same time, some historians have found themselves wondering if that was just an official "story" and whether Sheldon Street motorists are driving over graves.

THE LARK PIERCE MANHUNT

Walnut Grove was a very small community located southwest of Prescott in the nineteenth century. Even today, except for a few nearby ranches, it is largely a ghost town, accessible only by gravel roads. But in the 1880s, one of its residents was a man named Lark Pierce, who engaged in small ranching and mining, much like the majority of Arizona residents. But Lark Pierce was yet another individual who simply could not stay out of trouble.

Early on, the January 25, 1888 edition of the *Arizona Journal Miner* reported that Pierce had stabbed a man named McMillan, an employee of the Walnut Grove water storage company. McMillan survived, and Pierce was not prosecuted. That summer, though, the June 27 edition of the paper reported that Lark Pierce had entered the "cowboy tournament" that would be held in Prescott over the Fourth of July. This is significant in that, to this day, Prescott holds claim to hosting the world's oldest continuous rodeo, always held every year during the July Fourth festivities. The first year it was held was 1888, and Lark Pierce was apparently a contestant.

In early February 1889, a Walnut Grove resident named Edward Keyes was arrested for shooting to death an unidentified Mexican with whom he had been drinking and playing cards at Peter Verdier's saloon. Lark Pierce was originally named as being the only witness to the crime, but after an investigation, he was indicted as an accessory to the murder. This did not stick, as the grand jury in Prescott decided there was not enough evidence, and Pierce was freed.

By 1894, Lark Pierce had moved to the town of Congress, near Date Creek, where he opened a butcher shop. On March 20, 1894, local cattle merchants Oscar O'Neal and Hugo Richards (who ran a business called O'Neal and Richards) swore out a warrant, in Prescott, for Pierce's arrest for grand larceny, charging him with stealing a cow from them—just one cow. Yavapai County sheriff James Lowry put the warrant in the hands of his enthusiastic young deputy, a young man from Illinois named George C. Ruffner.

Deputy Ruffner headed for Congress with a horse and pack animal to arrest Pierce but, upon arriving, was told that the wanted man had left the area over a week earlier, clearly anticipating his arrest. As luck would have it, Ruffner encountered the famous camel driver known as Hi Jolly (he had been brought to Arizona years earlier by the U.S. Army in a failed, but still celebrated, experiment to turn camels into military pack animals in the Southwest). Hi Jolly told Ruffner he had seen an armed man with pack animals, matching Pierce's description, heading in the direction that would eventually lead to the Colorado River. Pierce had a head start of at least nine days, and any other lawman might have simply returned to Prescott. But Ruffner took off in the direction of California to try to track down the accused cattle thief.

As Ruffner approached Needles, California, a sandstorm came up and wiped out any tracks that might have belonged to Pierce. Still, the astute deputy concluded there was really only one logical place that Lark Pierce might go to hide, especially if he had come to realize he was being trailed: the Needles Mountains. Deputy Ruffner proceeded to hire a Chemehuevi Indian tracker to take him into the mountains. The guide told Ruffner there were only three springs in the mountains and that if the wanted man were fleeing in that direction, he would likely be at one of them. Arriving at the first spring, there were signs that a man, almost certainly Pierce, had camped there a few days but had moved on.

Arriving at the second spring, Deputy Ruffner saw from a distance that Lark Pierce was indeed camping there. Ruffner dismounted; threw his coat, stirrups and leathers over his horse to make it look like it was packed; and slowly moved in, walking behind the animal. Pierce quickly realized what was happening as Ruffner approached, but the deputy managed to draw his gun first and ordered Pierce to surrender. Now would begin the long journey back to Prescott (things like legal jurisdiction were seldom taken into account in those days).

Deputy George C. Ruffner handcuffed Pierce to himself, and they started the ride back. At night, when they had to camp, Ruffner made sure his guns and any rocks were out of Pierce's reach. Still, it was a dangerous proposition for the deputy to be alone with Pierce. It took them five days, but Ruffner brought his prisoner back to Prescott and lodged him in jail. Ruffner had been gone for two weeks and ridden over five hundred miles to bring in a man who had stolen one cow—the residents of Prescott were ecstatic at the realization that they had a deputy who would go to such lengths to "get his man."

Lark Pierce was arraigned and indicted by the grand jury on a charge of grand larceny. A trial was avoided when Pierce decided to plead guilty to the charge. He was sentenced to two years and nine months in Yuma Territorial Prison. He was pardoned by Arizona territorial governor Benjamin Franklin just before Thanksgiving Day 1896. The gesture was apparently made to restore Pierce's citizenship rights, as his full sentence was only a few days from ending and he would have been freed anyway. After being freed, Lark Pierce remained in Arizona; died on January 20, 1915, near Mesa; and was buried in the Mesa Cemetery. He was sixty-eight. His obituaries described him as a pioneer citizen and made no mention of his run-ins with the law.

The death certificate for small-time cattle rustler Lark Pierce, who died in Mesa in 1915. Years earlier, his apprehension put George C. Ruffner on track to become Yavapai County sheriff. *Arizona Department of Vital Records—public record.*

But for George C. Ruffner, the Lark Pierce case changed his life. Prescott was so impressed with his tenacity in the pursuit of the culprit that he was elected sheriff of Yavapai County outright in the elections of 1894. His behavior in that position continued to evoke praise and respect, and to this day, he remains one of Arizona's most admired lawmen. Because of this, the Pierce case in subsequent years has fallen into folklore, taking on some embellishments in the retelling that certainly were not so. Most notably, folklorists usually describe Lark Pierce as a "highwayman," making him sound more sinister than the petty cattle thief that he was. Also, folklore usually states that Ruffner disguised himself as an old Indian in order to sneak up on Pierce.

Murder at the Keystone

In the early 1890s, a young man named John Miller operated the Keystone Saloon in Prescott, with hotel rooms upstairs. The Keystone was located on Cortez Street, roughly one block from Whiskey Row. Business was good for Miller, until one day.

A stranger, Charles E. Hobart, rode into Prescott and rented a room from John Miller for four nights for one dollar. Hobart then reportedly "soiled" the room and the next morning demanded from Miller a refund of seventy-five cents for giving him a dirty room. After Miller refused, Hobart drew his rifle on the proprietor but then left. Angered, Miller called Prescott chief of police Steve Prince and had Hobart arrested. Brought before the justice of the peace, Hobart denied threatening Miller but was fined five dollars for being drunk and disorderly. It was Thursday.

That night, Hobart rented a horse from Joseph Dougherty and started visiting Whiskey Row saloons, including the Sazerac Saloon, as well as the famous Palace Saloon. In both places, Hobart started drunkenly telling people he was planning to kill Miller, but most of the patrons did not take him seriously. At the Sazerac, a man named John Ross took Hobart's threats more seriously and sent for Chief of Police Prince, who proceeded to head for the Keystone to warn Miller and to be there in case Hobart showed up.

But while this was going on, Hobart had left the Sazarac Saloon and, now liquored up enough to give himself the courage to carry out his threats, returned to the Keystone, where he once again demanded his money from John Miller. Without even giving his victim time to reply, Hobart drew his

Author Parker Anderson, dressed in period clothing, stands by the large gravestone for murdered bartender John Miller, who was shot to death by disgruntled customer Charles Hobart in 1895. *David Schmittinger.*

rifle and fired, killing Miller instantly. Hobart pointed his gun at two other witnesses in the saloon, William Sachs and Washington Roseberry, and ordered them to keep quiet. He then walked out of the Keystone Saloon, mounted his horse and rode off.

Hobart rode north on Cortez Street, turned left at Willis Street and then went down to Granite Street. There he rode down Granite Creek, where he was spotted by two men when he had difficulty getting his horse to ride under a bridge. After that, Hobart vanished.

Yavapai County sheriff George C. Ruffner and his deputies Joseph P. Dillon and Johnny Munds hit the trail almost immediately to find Hobart. The people of Prescott, outraged by the cold-blooded murder, threatened that, when Hobart was caught, they would storm the jail and lynch him. Prescott residents seemed to make this threat every time a terrible crime occurred, but there is no record that they ever attempted to make good on any of these threats. Hobart's horse returned to Dougherty's stable on its own a few hours later, walking into town from the east.

Sheriff Ruffner and his deputies trailed Charles Hobart to the town of Mayer, east of Prescott, after receiving word that the wanted man had been spotted buying bread from merchant James Hartsfield near there. Arriving in Mayer on Saturday, the lawmen figured that Hobart would try to make for Phoenix after darkness fell. Hiding out on the main road to Phoenix, Ruffner and his deputies waited in vain, but Hobart did not show. In actuality, Hobart was indeed planning to head for Phoenix but, in the dark of night, turned onto the wrong road and was going toward the Peck Mine in the Southern Bradshaw Mountains. The next morning, with the help of some Indian trackers, the lawmen struck Hobart's trail.

Arriving at the Cy Curtis Ranch near the Peck Mine, the lawmen concluded that Hobart was probably sleeping inside an abandoned building on the property. A miner from the Gladiator Mine was passing by, and the lawmen asked him to go up to the house to see if he could induce Hobart to come out. As the miner approached the house, Hobart came out on his own, armed with his rifle, and started asking the miner for directions. Sheriff Ruffner sprang out and ordered the wanted man to surrender. Hobart instead took aim at Ruffner when Joe Dillon ordered him to surrender from a different direction. Hobart again took aim, but Dillon fired his gun, hitting Hobart in the arm. Upon being wounded, the gunman surrendered. Compare this situation to today, when officers are now trained to open fire long before this.

Upon being lodged in the jail in Prescott, a doctor was sent for to cut the buckshot out of Hobart's arm. A reporter from the *Journal Miner* came and attempted to interview the accused murderer, but he would not say much except that he was "crazed with whiskey" on that fateful night.

Charles E. Hobart was indicted for first-degree murder. Judge John J. Hawkins appointed local attorneys Thomas G. Norris and H.T. Andrews to represent him, but Hobart claimed he did not want them or any lawyer. A plea of not guilty was entered on his behalf.

Hobart strenuously objected and repeatedly expressed his desire to plead guilty to the murder. Finally, Judge Hawkins allowed him to do so and set November 22, 1895, as the date for his sentencing. At that time, Hawkins sentenced Charles E. Hobart to life in Yuma Territorial Prison for the murder of John Miller instead of death by hanging.

The people of Prescott were outraged. Judge Hawkins explained that he was prohibited by law from imposing the death penalty on someone who had pleaded guilty to the crime. Prescott residents were angry that Hobart would probably get out before his life sentence was up. The *Arizona Journal Miner* wrote an angry editorial decrying Hobart's prison sentence in its November 27, 1895 issue and another one on December 11, 1895.

Sheriff George C. Ruffner took Charles Hobart to Yuma Territorial Prison, where he became prisoner no. 1113. There, he was a terrible prisoner. His surviving prison records show he was placed in solitary confinement eight times—three times for fighting, once for refusing to work, once for insubordination and three times for escape attempts. His prison record also shows, interestingly, that he had previously served time at the state prison of Michigan for an unspecified crime.

On August 29, 1909, Hobart was transferred to the new territorial prison in the town of Florence because of the closing of Yuma Territorial Prison. On May 1, 1912, he was paroled by Arizona governor George W.P. Hunt. He had served seventeen years of his life sentence—longer than some had predicted, but in the end, the critics of the judicial system in 1895 were correct. Charles Hobart did not finish his life sentence and walked out of the state prison at Florence a free man. His fate is unknown.

One interesting side note: the building that housed the Keystone Saloon was regarded as cursed. According to the October 30, 1895 *Journal Miner*, it had been the site of no fewer than three suicides over the years, and lightning once struck a barn attached to it, killing two horses.

THE PARKER STORY

One of the most famous and notorious criminal cases in Prescott history actually began in Visalia, California, in Tulare County. There, in 1865, Fleming Parker was born to a small stock farmer and his wife. He had three sisters, but Parker was orphaned by the time he was fourteen, his mother having died in childbirth with another baby and his father committing suicide shortly thereafter. Young Parker was then raised by his maternal grandfather, Fleming Work, who valiantly carried on the impossible task of keeping the wild young man out of trouble.

In 1885, Parker and a partner named Philo Johns apparently tried to start up a small cattle-rustling business and were arrested for stealing a steer. In exchange for a lighter sentence, Johns agreed to testify against his partner Parker, who was then sentenced to a term in San Quentin Prison.

When Parker got out of prison, he and another friend named Walter Brown were arrested for stealing wheat out of a Tulare County farmer's barn. Once again, Parker's partner turned on him in exchange for leniency, and Parker was convicted on Brown's testimony and returned to San Quentin.

This time, Parker's attorney appealed to the California Supreme Court and successfully got the conviction overturned on a technicality. Upon being released from San Quentin for this reason, Fleming Parker saddled up and headed for Arizona, where maybe he could put his past behind him and where he was also out of the reach of his attorney, whom he never paid for getting him out of prison. In Arizona, Parker changed his first name to James, or Jim, for his new start. With the exception of one wanted poster, Parker was never again publicly referred to as Fleming in his lifetime.

In Arizona, Jim Parker sought work as a ranch hand. His skill with horses led him to be a much-sought-after cowboy on the ranches of Northern Arizona. It has often been said that, during this time (the mid-1890s), Parker befriended another young cowboy named George C. Ruffner. Parker and Ruffner are said to have drifted around from ranch to ranch together, drinking and having fun, but they would later part company. George Ruffner settled down to become a respected businessman in Prescott. Parker, on the other hand, was interested in obtaining his money through quicker and less scrupulous methods.

Parker headed farther north, where he took up with the Abe Thompson Gang, a small group of petty thieves and cattle rustlers who had terrorized the ranchers and settlers near Peach Springs, Arizona (in Mohave County), for several years. The gang's mercurial leader was Abe Thompson, a former lawman who switched sides following his wife's death in 1893. In addition to Parker, other gang members included Love Marvin, Jim Williams aka Harry Williams (Williams's true identity remains unknown) and several Mexicans and "half-breeds."

It was a cold, dark, snowy night on February 8, 1897. The Thompson Gang, probably under the sociopathic influence of Parker, had tired of cattle rustling and sought bigger game—they made plans to rob an overland Atlantic & Pacific train that ran near Peach Springs on its way to Los Angeles. What the bandits hoped to get out of the robbery is unknown, although a legend contends that the train was carrying a shipment of gold that night.

Abe Thompson and Love Marvin went into Peach Springs, where they proceeded to whoop it up and make themselves conspicuous, giving the impression to the townspeople that the whole gang was in town that night. Meanwhile, Parker and "Williams" selected the spot for the train robbery: a treacherous curve in a rock cut that was deemed so hazardous that the railroad employed watchmen to stand there all day and all night to make sure the trains got through with no trouble (what a thankless job that must have been). The two bandits ambushed the watchman and forced him to flag the train down to a stop.

At that point, Parker demanded at gunpoint that the train's fireman uncouple the engine and mail car from the rest of the train and take the engine and mail car down the track to Nelson siding. In the confusion of the ill-planned robbery, an express messenger managed to shoot and kill "Williams." Parker, who was rifling the mail car, was apparently unaware of this when it happened.

This is the best-known photo of Yavapai County sheriff George C. Ruffner, taken in 1897, the year he was put in the difficult position of tracking down his old friend Jim Parker for murder. *Sharlot Hall Museum.*

The mail car was a strange target for a holdup, and whatever the bandits hoped to find was not there. Parker, realizing he was out of time, hurriedly grabbed some fistfuls of mail and took off. Later, several pounds of dynamite and blasting caps were found on "Williams's" body, indicating the bandits were somehow expecting to find a safe or a vault.

With Parker's partner dead and no loot to show for any of it, the Rock Cut Train Robbery (as it came to be known) had been totally botched, so badly that it spelled the end of the Abe Thompson Gang. Thompson and Marvin were quickly arrested as accessories to the robbery, and Parker now found himself on the run from three different county posses: Mohave, Coconino and Yavapai. He was eventually snuck up on and apprehended by his one-time friend George C. Ruffner, who had since become sheriff of Yavapai County. After some dispute among the three sheriffs over who had jurisdiction over the case, Ruffner won out, took Parker to Prescott and lodged him in the Yavapai County Jail, where he shared a cell with Thompson, Marvin and a few other criminals, including Louis C. Miller.

Remember Louis C. Miller? He was the Prescott constable who shot the chief of police a few chapters back. Now, the man who couldn't stay out of trouble was in jail awaiting trial for forging a check and in the same cell with Parker. Trouble was inevitable, and in May 1897, jailor Robert Meador responded to cries for water from the prisoners. When he opened the cell door, he was overpowered by a Mexican inmate, Cornelia Sarata, who was in jail for an attempted murder in Crown King. While Meador and Sarata were struggling, Parker and Miller ran to a storeroom and grabbed several rifles. When the three escapees started to flee the jail, they were confronted by deputy district attorney Lee Norris, who came down to investigate the commotion. In the heat of the moment, Parker shot him on the spot, and Norris died that night after lingering for several hours.

Look Out for
Train Robber and Murderer.

$1000 REWARD

For the Arrest and Conviction of

FLEMING PARKER

Who escaped from County Jail at Prescott, Arizona, on or about May 13, 1897. In making his escape he shot and mortally wounded the Deputy District Attorney.

DESCRIPTION.

Fleming Parker, alias William Parker, is now about 31 years of age; 5 feet 7½ inches high; weighs 165 lbs.; light grey eyes; brown hair; size of foot 6½ inches; teeth in fair condition; high, full forehead; round features; straight nose; small mouth; round chin; vacine mark on left forearm; mole back of neck; scar on left side of head. Usually wears his hat on back of his head; is a cowboy by occupation, and a native of Tulare County. His picture as given hereon is a perfect likeness of him. He has served a term of five years in San Quentin for burglary. When last heard of he was heading for Nevada or Utah; had a repeating rifle with him. He was arrested for attempting to rob the A. & P. R. R. train at Peach Springs, Arizona, and was being held for trial in the Prescott Jail when he escaped. His partner Jim, alias Harry Williams of Utah, was killed at the time of the attempted robbery. There is no doubt of his conviction if captured. If arrested telegraph Sheriff Ruffner, Prescott, Arizona, or the undersigned.

J. N. THACKER,

SPECIAL OFFICER, WELLS, FARGO & CO.,

SAN FRANCISCO

SAN FRANCISCO, May 18, 1897.

This is the wanted poster that was issued for Fleming "Jim" Parker after the jailbreak in which he gunned down the deputy district attorney, Lee Norris. *Sharlot Hall Museum.*

The three escapees ran across the street to a livery stable owned by Sheriff Ruffner, where they held up the handler and grabbed two horses. Parker took Sheriff Ruffner's prize white gelding, Sure-Shot, and this caused as much controversy in old Prescott as the murder of Lee Norris. There was speculation that no one fired a shot at the fleeing fugitives because they were afraid of hitting the sheriff's horse. Parker was on Sure-Shot while Miller and Sarata rode the other horse.

Posses were instantly formed, and they caught up with the fleeing bandits at Lynx Creek, where a gunfight erupted. Surviving details of this firefight are contradictory, but Miller was wounded, Parker hoisted him up on Sure-Shot and they rode off. Why the posse members would let them ride off so easily is unknown, but again, it may have been due to fear that a stray bullet might hit the sheriff's horse.

At some point, the outlaws split up. The wounded Louis C. Miller later surrendered to authorities at the home of his sister in Jerome, while Cornelia Sarata was never seen again, dead or alive. He had been wounded in the jailbreak by a shot fired by jailor Meador, so he may have crawled away and died somewhere. Others believe he made it to Mexico. There is no evidence either way.

Parker led his pursuers on a long chase through the Kaibab-Williams area, where he had many friends among the country settlers who distrusted "city folk" and who were willing to help him elude the posse. He was also quite resourceful, at one point abusing Sure-Shot by removing his horseshoes and putting them on backwards to make the tracks look like they were going in the other direction.

But Parker's luck eventually ran out. He made it as far as a trading post on the Navajo Indian Reservation near Tuba City, where he stopped for food. The white trader Samuel S. Preston recognized Parker from his wanted poster that was being circulated and rounded up several Indian trackers. They snuck up on Parker while he was sleeping and took him without incident.

Back in jail in Prescott, Fleming "James" Parker went on trial for the first-degree murder of Lee Norris. His court-appointed attorneys argued that there was no premeditation for the crime, so the charge should have been second-degree murder or voluntary manslaughter. But in the end, Parker was convicted and sentenced to hang.

Surprisingly, Parker's attorneys did not walk away after the conviction, as many often did in those days, and they appealed his death sentence. The appeals delayed the execution for over a year, but after the Arizona Territorial Supreme Court upheld his conviction and death sentence, it was over. On

This photo of Sheriff Ruffner's prize white horse, Sure-Shot, was taken after he was recovered following his theft by Jim Parker after the jailbreak. *Sharlot Hall Museum.*

June 3, 1898, Parker mounted the gallows on the east side of the courthouse in Prescott. In his last words, he stated that he did not believe he deserved to be hanged but that he bore no ill will toward anyone. He was very calm and collected as the deputies strapped and pinioned him, something that unnerved a lot of people.

Sheriffs were still required to officiate at hangings, so the switch was pulled by Sheriff George C. Ruffner himself. After Parker's body was cut down, Ruffner himself drove the hearse to the Potter's Field in Citizens Cemetery. The location of his grave is known, but there is no marker and likely never was. They buried him beside Dilda. Fleming "James" Parker was the eighth of the eleven men legally hanged in Yavapai County between 1875 and 1925.

The Parker story is one of Prescott's best-known legends. It continues to fascinate the historians of old Prescott and devotees of western lore. For many years afterward, old-timers would boast that it was actually they who had captured Parker. Numerous myths and folklore have sprung up over the years concerning the case. Probably the best known is that Parker asked for

Above: The hanging of outlaw and murderer Fleming "James" Parker on June 3, 1898. He was the calmest person on the gallows and faced his death with enough bravery that it unnerved some people. *Sharlot Hall Museum.*

Left: Parker is hanged. *Sharlot Hall Museum.*

a visit from his favorite Prescott prostitute the night before he was hanged. People love that story for God knows what reason, but there is no evidence to support it. It was also asserted countless times over the years that Parker was Butch Cassidy's brother—which is not even remotely true.

George C. Ruffner's
Bad Week

Yavapai County sheriff George C. Ruffner was having a very bad week. On June 3, 1898, he had pulled the switch at the hanging of his old friend Fleming Parker. Three days later, on June 6, 1898, the still and quiet of everyday Prescott was shattered by the sound of gunfire on North Cortez Street in Prescott. Soon, Dr. John Bryan McNally, one of Prescott's most prominent physicians (and remembered today as a great Prescott pioneer), staggered out of his office into the street with a gunshot wound. It was nothing short of a miracle that McNally was alive, for, as the *Journal Miner* reported, "The bullet struck a watch in Dr. McNally's pocket, glancing off and then passed through the fleshy part of the left arm between the elbow and the wrist."

Dr. McNally said that he had been shot by a deranged prospector named Frank Stewart in a dispute over a bill of five dollars. Stewart, who would later be officially identified as A.A. Stewart (both names were probably phony), had escaped toward the Verde Valley but would later double back toward the Hassayampa River. Sheriff Ruffner, still recovering from the Parker hanging, formed a posse and struck the trail of A.A. Stewart.

On the run from the law, Stewart proved to be as resourceful and vicious as Parker had been. At one point, Sheriff Ruffner sent an Indian tracker ahead of him. The Indian later returned on foot, having been bushwhacked and his horse stolen by Stewart. The insane prospector also shot and wounded a country settler named William Deering and stole his horse. Then, when that horse tired out as well, Stewart stole one from a country slaughterhouse, all the while staying ahead of the posse.

Left: A portrait of Dr. John Bryan McNally, the pioneer Prescott doctor who was shot by a deranged patient in 1898 but whose pocket watch kept him from being killed. *Sharlot Hall Museum.*

Below: This is the watch, damaged by a bullet, that prevented Dr. John Bryan McNally from being killed by the patient who shot him. The watch is today owned by Gerald McNally (the doctor's grandson), and this photo appears here with his kind permission. *Alan Krause.*

Stewart also broke into a number of cabins along the way, presumably looking for food. His trail was easy to follow, as he wore a pair of uncommon hobnailed shoes. At one point, Sheriff Ruffner went on ahead of the posse and came across Stewart, who proceeded to escape in a hail of gunfire, with one bullet actually passing through the sheriff's hat, according to the *Journal Miner*. Sheriff Ruffner reportedly kept that hat on display in his office for the rest of his life.

After several days without food or sleep, A.A. Stewart had had enough. He stopped a country settler and told him to go inform the Ruffner posse that he was ready to surrender; he couldn't go on any further. After being taken into custody, Stewart told Deputy Jeff Davis that one night he had Davis in point-blank range but didn't shoot when he realized the deputy was not alone.

A.A. Stewart was convicted of attempted murder and sentenced to fifteen years in Yuma Territorial Prison. There, he was a troublesome inmate. He was repeatedly put in solitary confinement for assaulting and threatening prison guards and once for digging a hole in his jail cell. At one point, he was judged insane and sent to an insane asylum but was later returned to the Yuma prison.

On November 10, 1900, A.A. Stewart escaped from Yuma Territorial Prison using a rope ladder he had somehow acquired or made. He was never seen again, despite an extensive manhunt. Two prison guards were fired for negligence over the incident.

If this story sounds familiar to some readers, it is because a somewhat different version of it exists in Prescott-area folklore. In that version, the shooter's name is inexplicably changed to "Bugger Bennett," with other things in the story changed as well. This folklore version seems to have originated in a wildly inaccurate biography of George C. Ruffner, written by pulp writers Robert and Toni McInnes for a long-defunct periodical, *Sheriff Magazine*. It has since been widely repeated in that form, although a thorough check of criminal records of the period shows that no one named Bennett was ever indicted for shooting a doctor during George Ruffner's time as sheriff. The "Bugger Bennett" legend is unquestionably derived from the story of A.A. Stewart.

As for Dr. John Bryan McNally, he continued his successful medical practice in Prescott until his death in 1928. One has to wonder how many nights of sleep he lost over the years, wondering if the psychotic prospector was coming back for him.

THE GODDARD
STATION MURDERS

In the late nineteenth and early twentieth centuries, Goddard Station was a popular stagecoach stop on the road between Phoenix and Prescott. It was located about where Black Canyon City is today and was operated by Charles E. Goddard and his wife, Rosa.

On February 1, 1903, two men described by witnesses as heavy-set Mexicans walked in and asked to be fed. Then they proceeded to draw their guns and open fire. When the dust had settled, Goddard and his clerk, Frank Cox, lay dead. Witnessing the deadly attack were Rosa Goddard and a friend named Milton Turnbull. The murderers made no attempt to rob the place, and the motive for the killings remains unknown to this day.

As noted earlier in this book, attitudes against Mexicans were generally hostile in those days. Newspapers of the era reflected these conditions, regaling the public with countless incidents of crimes allegedly committed by Mexicans. Some of them were undoubtedly guilty, while others certainly had the misfortune to be in the wrong place at the wrong time.

The Goddard Station killers got away, and when word reached Prescott, Yavapai County sheriff Joe Roberts set out in pursuit. He was unsuccessful, as the two men safely made it across the Mexican border. This seemed to end the case.

A short time later, a Maricopa County deputy named Billy Blankenship was informed that two Mexicans matching the descriptions of the killers were working on a railroad section just across the Mexican border. How he acquired this kind of detailed information is unknown, yet he went to the border and persuaded the section boss to cooperate in a sting operation to capture the two men.

The section boss then sent one of the suspected men across the American line on a team, where he was quickly nabbed. The accused killer did not even know he had crossed back into America—the border was neither fenced nor guarded in those days, and only law enforcement officials from both sides knew where the line was. The boss paid the second suspect's wages with a check drawn on an American bank in Naco (in Cochise County), and when the suspect tried to sneak across the border to cash it, Deputy Blankenship was waiting for him.

The two Mexicans were identified as Hilario Hidalgo and Francisco Renteria. Sheriff Roberts wasted no time in going to Naco to claim the prisoners. Hidalgo and Renteria were lodged in the Yavapai County Jail in Prescott, where they were identified as the Goddard Station murderers by Turnbull and also by Francisco Rodriguez, a shepherd who claimed to have conversed with the men outside Goddard Station just before the shooting.

Hidalgo and Renteria were brought to trial in June 1903. Their court-appointed attorney produced one alibi witness, Jacinto Cota, who swore on the stand that the two men were out drinking with him on Prescott's Whiskey Row at the time of the murders. The jury did not buy this, and the accused killers were swiftly convicted and sentenced to hang. As usual, their attorneys walked away from the case then, so they could not file any appeals. They never admitted their guilt, which unnerved Prescott townspeople, who were shaken to see anyone going to meet their maker with a lie on their lips. The Roman Catholic priest who was present at Parker's execution, Father Alfred Quetu, warned the men that they could not expect any mercy from God if they did not confess their guilt and repent before they died. Both men refused.

On July 31, 1903, Hilario Hidalgo and Francisco Renteria were hanged on the east side of the courthouse, which had become the usual execution spot. As Sheriff Roberts pulled the switch, their final words were simply, "Adios!"

Considering the racial atmosphere of the day, it is reasonable to ask: were they really guilty? Probably, but were they treated with the same rights and privileges as other murderers? No.

A number of later accounts of this case refer to it as an example of how swift frontier justice really was. Scarcely six months had passed between the murders and the executions. But Hidalgo and Renteria were the first hangings in Yavapai County since Parker five years earlier. During that time, quite a few murderers had their sentences commuted by higher courts and territorial governors. In fact, so many killers escaped the gallows in

Above: Convicted murderers Hilario Hidalgo and Francisco Renteria kneel in prayer on the gallows before being hanged in 1903. *Sharlot Hall Museum.*

Left: Showing the different attitudes of the era, photos of the hanging of Hidalgo and Renteria were later sold on postcards, albeit with an erroneous date of 1904 (it was actually 1903). *Sharlot Hall Museum.*

Arizona during this period that newspapers openly complained about it.

The motive for the horrible crime was never known. The murderers made no attempt to rob the station after gunning down Goddard and Cox. In pure speculation, some historians have surmised that it was due to some kind of grudge, or perhaps a hired hit, but no one ever knew for sure.

Prescott's Mexican community, in sympathy with their brothers, took up a collection for the funeral and burial of the two in unmarked graves in Citizens Cemetery, right beside Parker, who in turn had been buried beside Dilda, making this a sort of "hangman's row."

Reflecting the attitudes of the era, the newspapers seldom referred to the two killers by name—they were simply referred to as "the Mexicans." In fact, the racial attitudes are best reflected by the July 28, 1903 *Journal Miner*, which contemptuously reported, "It is said that when the guards

A piece of the noose from the double hanging of Hilario Hidalgo and Francisco Renteria. It was traditional in those days for participants of a hanging to cut up the noose into sections so each individual would have a souvenir. This section is now reposited at Sharlot Hall Museum, where it was recently displayed as part of a 2015 law and order exhibit. *Sharlot Hall Museum.*

compelled them to take a bath last night, they showed more signs of real suffering than at any previous time since they have been in jail."

THE PERJURY TRIAL OF JACINTO COTA

Also reflecting the racial attitudes of the era was a long-forgotten second criminal case to arise out of the trial of Hilario Hidalgo and Francisco

Renteria. Remember previously, their attorney provided one alibi witness, Jacinto Cota, who testified under oath that the two accused murderers were out drinking with him in Prescott at the time of the murders.

Sheriff Joe Roberts was outraged that anyone would try to save the murderers, so he angrily swore out a warrant for the arrest of Cota on a charge of perjury, or lying under oath (which remains a felony today but is seldom prosecuted). The legal rationale for such a charge is this: if a defendant is found guilty of a crime by a jury, it is legal proof that contrary alibi witnesses perjured themselves. Cota was quickly arrested and lodged in the Yavapai County Jail in Prescott.

Surprisingly, Cota's court-appointed attorney fought hard for him, arguing that Cota's infraction of the law, even if true, had not harmed society. He succeeded in getting Cota's original indictment quashed on a legal technicality after the trial had started. The jury, already sworn, was discharged from the case while the authorities tried to decide what to do next.

Sheriff Roberts pressed the case hard, and Cota was re-indicted almost immediately. A new jury was sworn in, and Jacinto Cota was tried and convicted of perjury in December 1903. He was sentenced to four years at Yuma Territorial Prison. It was an unusually harsh sentence considering the nature of the crime.

So the questions must be asked: would Cota have drawn such a stiff sentence if he had not been a Mexican? Would he have even been indicted at all if he had been white? Perjury was not prosecuted very often in those days and still isn't. Yes, it is likely that Hidalgo and Renteria were truly guilty of murder, thus making Cota guilty of perjury. But even if this is so, Cota's punishment did not fit the crime.

Jacinto Cota was released from Yuma Territorial Prison in 1906, three years into his sentence. After that, he disappeared, never to be heard from again. As he was close to the border in Yuma, he probably crossed over into Mexico and stayed there. If he did indeed commit perjury, he undoubtedly did so in a belief that he was helping his "brothers" against white man's justice. And given the social atmosphere of the time, who could blame him for thinking that?

A Long Life of Trouble

Frank Spence owned and worked a small ranch west of Prescott. While most ranchers were (and still are) hardworking, industrious and respectable people, Spence had a bad reputation in Prescott. He was known to get drunk fairly regularly and threaten people while in this condition. He also had numerous run-ins with the law. Little is known of his past, except that he had previously worked as a miner around Tombstone and Bisbee, in Cochise County, before heading up to Yavapai County.

In February 1903, when he was well into his fifties, Frank Spence was arrested for shooting a Prescott printer named "Shorty" Simmons. Simmons survived, and Spence miraculously avoided any serious jail time. Again, on March 7, 1905, a drunken Spence encountered a Prescott resident named William Thomas, whose wagon was stuck in the mud. According to Thomas, he asked Spence for help, but Spence instead drew his gun and fired two shots at him. Thomas swore out a warrant for Spence's arrest, but Spence claimed he fired his gun to frighten Thomas's horses into making an extra effort to get out of the mud. As it was just a case of one man's word against another's, the grand jury opted not to indict Spence.

The troubled life of Frank Spence came to a head on October 22, 1908. Late that day, Spence arrived in Prescott and turned himself in to Yavapai County sheriff James R. Lowry. He claimed he had killed a man named Edgar Sullivan in self-defense out at his ranch. Spence claimed that Sullivan, about whom little is known, came at him with a butcher knife and that he shot him in the head.

Upon arriving at Spence's cabin, deputy sheriff John Merritt, district attorney Robert E. Morrison, Dr. Robert N. Looney and mortician Lester Ruffner examined the scene and held a coroner's inquest. Sullivan's body was lying face down in a pool of blood with a butcher knife under the corpse's hand. But the officials determined that the situation was not as Spence had claimed. Dr. Looney proclaimed that Edgar Sullivan had been shot in the back of the head by a large-caliber bullet, showing that he had not been facing his assailant. The doctor and Lester Ruffner also determined that Sullivan had apparently fallen into the fireplace upon being shot, as parts of his face and hair were singed and these were not gunpowder burns. The dead man's hand was clenched, but not around the handle of the butcher knife. It was decided that Spence had placed the knife under the hand to corroborate his story.

Following the investigation, Frank Spence was charged with first-degree murder in the death of Edgar Sullivan. As for a motive, apparently Spence had quietly sold his ranch to Sullivan, probably while intoxicated, and then refused to move out. Supposedly, the two men lived together on the ranch for a short time trying to settle their dispute, and it ended in murder.

Spence went on trial around December 2, 1908. He was represented in court by attorney James Loy. When Dr. Robert N. Looney took the stand, he testified that Sullivan had clearly been shot in the back of the head because the entrance wound was smaller than the exit wound. Under cross-examination, attorney Loy pointed to U.S. government statistics (compiled during the Civil War) that claimed that gunshot wounds actually leave larger entrance holes than exit holes. Looney would not concede this, claiming that all textbooks on gunshot wounds invariably show that the entrance wound is smaller than an exit wound. Attorney Loy did force Looney to admit that he personally was largely unfamiliar with gunshot wounds made from steel-jacketed bullets, the kind used in the Sullivan murder.

Lester Ruffner took the stand and repeated his testimony that Sullivan had fallen into the fireplace face first after being shot. He apparently had been sitting at a table eating when Spence put a gun to his head and pulled the trigger.

Frank Spence was quickly convicted of murder and sentenced to death. The date of his hanging was set for February 5, 1909. He bitterly complained that his trial had been unfair and biased and that the authorities were using this to eliminate him, as he had been such a problem in Prescott over the years. He defiantly maintained his story that he had shot Sullivan in self-defense after Sullivan came at him with a butcher knife.

There would be delays in carrying out Spence's execution. The condemned man's nephew arrived in Prescott from Salisbury, Missouri, and hired a new attorney, Richard P. Talbot, to appeal his uncle's case to higher courts. When February 1909 rolled around, Spence was granted a stay of execution while the Arizona Territorial Supreme Court reviewed his appeal. For reasons unknown, this appeal took longer than usual for those days. In April 1910, the high court upheld the conviction and death sentence of Frank Spence for the murder of Edgar Sullivan.

(On a side note, on November 2, 1909, while Spence was awaiting the results of his appeal, another man was found dead in Spence's old cabin where Sullivan had been murdered. William L. Bent, a tuberculosis patient from Buffalo, New York, had taken up residence there only a few days earlier. His death was attributed to heart disease compounded by his TB.)

Following the failure of Spence's appeals, his execution date was reset for August 5, 1910. There was much excitement in Prescott, and this would be the town's first hanging since the executions of Hilario Hidalgo and Francisco Renteria in 1903. The condemned man reportedly grew very afraid of his impending death and unwaveringly stuck to his story of self-defense. He reportedly stopped eating and grew emaciated very quickly. Yavapai County sheriff Smith began preparations for the hanging and decided to use a large room in the basement of the courthouse, near the jail cells, for the event, instead of having it on the east side of the courthouse as had been usually done. The Yavapai County Board of Supervisors ordered the rope that would be used in Spence's hanging.

But it was not to be. Very shortly before the execution was to take place, territorial governor Richard E. Sloan commuted Spence's sentence to life imprisonment. The citizens of Prescott were outraged, and despite his fear of hanging, Spence himself expressed disappointment, saying that he would have preferred death over spending the rest of his life in prison, caged like an animal. He predicted he would die within two years in prison and continued to maintain his innocence in the Sullivan murder, claiming it was self-defense.

Sheriff Smith took Frank Spence to the Arizona Territorial Prison in Florence, Arizona (the prison at Yuma having been closed by the territory the previous year).

While in prison, the aging Frank Spence suffered a stroke that rendered him partially paralyzed. At one point, he was offered a parole, probably out of sympathy, but he declined it, stating that in his infirm condition, it would be better for him to remain in prison.

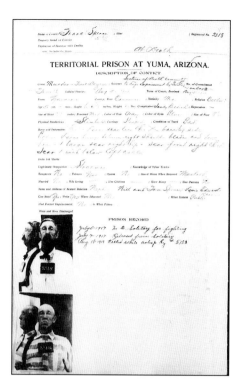

Left: The official prison record for murderer Frank Spence, from the Arizona Territorial Prison in Florence (though they were clearly still using old Yuma Prison forms). He was murdered by another inmate in 1918. *Arizona State Library and Archives.*

Below: Edgar Sullivan, who was murdered in 1908 by Frank Spence, is buried in Citizens Cemetery in a grave marked only by a small ring of stones. *David Schmittinger.*

On August 18, 1918, Frank Spence was sleeping in the prison yard when another inmate, Miguel Grijalva, repeatedly bashed his head in with a baseball bat he had somehow gotten his hands on. Death was believed to be almost instantaneous for Spence. No motive was determined for Grijalva's attack except that he was mentally ill and simply saw an opportunity to attack someone. Spence was buried in the prison cemetery at Florence.

As for Spence's victim, Edgar Sullivan, he was buried in Citizens Cemetery in Prescott in an unmarked grave. Oddly, when adding his name to the existing map of the cemetery, his name was erroneously misspelled "Edna" Sullivan—quite a typographical error. Because of this, knowledge of the final resting place for Edgar Sullivan was lost for many decades until Yavapai Cemetery Association president Pat Atchison and I discovered the error and established that burial site as the final resting place of murder victim Edgar Sullivan.

OMBRE MUERTE ON
THUMB BUTTE

Arguably the most famous and visible landmark in Prescott is Thumb Butte, a large rocky mountain that overlooks the city and can be seen from virtually every vantage point. Unfortunately, this striking mountain has been the scene of several tragic accidents and at least one unsolved murder over the years. Many of these incidents are recent phenomena, but Thumb Butte has always had its share of tragedies. Take the following story, for instance:

On January 22, 1911, two young men, Roy Richards and Henry Brinkmeyer Jr., went mountain climbing on Thumb Butte. Near the top, they happened to glance down into a hidden and deep crevice and were shocked to see the still, decayed form of a man at the bottom. They ran back to Prescott as fast as they could for help. Soon, justice of the peace and coroner Charles McLane, accompanied by a coroner's jury and Lester Ruffner, the undertaker (and brother of former and also future sheriff George C. Ruffner), made their way to the crevice. The dead man's coat and vest were hanging from a nearby tree. In the pockets were a pair of eyeglasses, a comb, scissors, a small horn whistle and a box of quinine tablets—nothing that gave any clue to the dead man's identity.

The descent down to the body was highly treacherous and was accomplished by McLane, Ruffner and Wiley Woodruff. When they reached the body, lying beside a cactus growing in the crevice, they confirmed the man was dead and that the body had probably been lying there undetected for at least five months.

The majestic mountain of Thumb Butte, taken in the early twentieth century. Overlooking Prescott, it can be seen from virtually all vantage points in the city. *Sharlot Hall Museum.*

They further determined that the man had climbed down into the spot by himself and committed suicide. A Smith and Wesson handgun was lying by his side, next to a small mirror. A note was found in a small tin shaving box in his pocket that read: "This is as fine a place for a dead man as Cecil Rhodes has in the Matabele Hills, so I will take a rest here. I hope they won't disturb me. My life is just as thorny as this cactus. Therefore I want to quite [*sic*] this Devil's Kingdom. My spirit will go where there is a better Ruler. OMBRE MUERTE."

He had simply signed the note "Dead Man" (in Spanish) and gave no clue to his identity. As the crevice was so well hidden, it was clear the man had intentionally chosen it for his tomb.

McLane, Ruffner and Woodruff decided that removing the body would be exceedingly difficult, requiring someone to lift it out of the crevice and lower it three hundred feet to the nearest trail. Therefore, they decided to leave him where he was, as it was unlikely many more people would discover him since he had hidden himself so well.

Back in Prescott, the Yavapai County Board of Supervisors was horrified by this decision and ordered the removal of the body from Thumb Butte. Heavy rains in Prescott delayed the operation for several weeks, but finally, Lester Ruffner and a small crew brought the body down from the suicide's chosen tomb. He was laid to rest in an unmarked grave in Citizens Cemetery in the Potter's Field section, where the poor and undesirable were buried at county expense.

So who was the Thumb Butte suicide? We will never know. If he had family or relatives anywhere, they never knew what happened to their loved one.

Thumb Butte has been the scene of a number of tragic events over the years. Rumors abound to this day about ghosts and other strange phenomena on the Butte, and many will caution you not to go exploring or hiking there at night.

Will Morfia from the Air in a Small Jar

In September 1912, miner Robert Meador was working his claims near the Senator Mine some miles southeast of Prescott in the Southern Bradshaw Mountains. Meador had been a longtime pioneer resident of Yavapai County and had a string of bad luck where he happened to be in the wrong place at the wrong time. Years before, among other incidents, he was the jailor who was ambushed by outlaw Fleming Parker and two cohorts, the story of which was told in "The Parker Story." Since that time, Meador had several other unfortunate instances where he found bodies out in the country or was in the middle of things when a fight broke out.

On a fine autumn day in 1912, Meador discovered a corpse lying under some oak brush. A gun was found beside the corpse, and a suicide note was found in his coat pocket. The body was in an advanced state of decay, and when coroner Charles McLane and undertaker Lester Ruffner made their examination of the remains, they concluded that he had been dead for at least six months.

The suicide note indicated that the dead man had been a practitioner of spiritism and that his obsession with these beliefs had driven him insane:

Will Morfia from the air in a small jar. Mind within me, I am obliged to commit suicide to avoid a brutal attack by the spirits from the spirit world. When you leave my body, through the bullet hole in my head, and come into conscious being, will—by an effort of the will—that I wake up so that I, as you—both in one—may fly to some very distant point, probably South

This is the suicide note left by Malcolm Matheson in his own handwriting. Among other things, he believed he was being tormented by evil spirits. *Arizona State Library and Archives.*

America, where we have often had to escape, and that, too, without delay. Do not speak to the spirit voices around my head, and if you see spirits, silence them by the power of your will.

The note was signed Malcolm Matheson.

After Matheson was found, miners from the nearby areas came forward and confirmed what the suicide note implied—that Matheson was not all right in the head and that he talked incoherently about spirits and how they helped him locate mines of great wealth. He also was prone to walking around at night, making noise and talking to himself, keeping the other miners awake.

The miners believed that Matheson had family in California, and Lester Ruffner succeeded in locating a brother and sister of the deceased. The family requested that he be buried in Prescott, so the troubled and tortured Malcolm Matheson was laid to rest in an unmarked grave in Citizens Cemetery. But as he could not rest in life, he was also not allowed to rest in peace. As seen in "The Blue Dick," in the 1960s, Sheldon Street in Prescott was widened, and four rows of graves were wiped out to accommodate this. Matheson's grave was one of them. All of these bodies were reportedly reburied in a mass grave in Rolling Hills Cemetery near the small Prescott Airport.

ELKS OPERA HOUSE

Another famous landmark of Prescott is the Elks Opera House on Gurley Street, about one block east of the Courthouse Plaza. It was built by the Elks Lodge in Prescott, No. 330 BPOE. This theater opened on February 20, 1905, and has had a long and storied history as a performing arts facility and movie theater. In the 110 years of its existence, there has been no prolonged period when it was ever closed. In 2010, thanks to fundraising and a large grant from the Harold James Foundation, the opera house was lovingly and painstakingly remodeled and restored to its original historical grandeur.

Needless to say, in its rich history, there have been some interesting events at the Elks Opera House. In 1912, the Elks had entered a period where they were booking vaudeville acts and motion picture shorts. Vaudeville was big in America at this time, much bigger than many remember, especially since so many modern historians regard vaudeville with derision. In addition to vaudeville, the Elks management also retained some local performers.

One of these local performers was a violinist named Professor Stanislaus Scherzel, a Russian immigrant. While he was on a vaudeville tour, he had been booked temporarily at the Elks in Prescott. When he expressed an interest in staying in town, Elks manager Ed Dillon hired him to play the violin every night before the movies were shown. Professor Scherzel became very popular with regular audience members at the Elks.

But sadly, all was not well with Professor Scherzel, who was subject to fits of depression. As with many depression cases down to the present day,

The Elks Opera House on Gurley Street in Prescott is seen here circa the 1930s. It opened in 1905 and remains the oldest continuously operating theater facility in Arizona. *Sharlot Hall Museum.*

The interior of the Elks Opera House as it looked shortly after opening in 1905. After decades of misguided remodeling, in 2010, it was restored to almost its original appearance. *Sharlot Hall Museum.*

friends and acquaintances of the depressed individual often do not recognize the warning signs until it is too late.

On August 25, 1912, Professor Scherzel was walking home, accompanied by a friend, Fred Ellis. He made a social stop at the office of the *Journal Miner* newspaper, where he shot the breeze with his friends for a few minutes and then continued on home. Fred Ellis and everyone else he came in contact with that afternoon all said later that he was in good spirits.

Upon arriving home, accompanied by Ellis, Professor Scherzel became embroiled in an argument with his wife. Embarrassed, Ellis was about to make a fast exit when he heard a gunshot. Scherzel had gone into another room and put a bullet through his heart. He was thirty-seven years old.

In the days that followed, some of Scherzel's friends realized that he had previously displayed signs of suicidal depression, but they did not recognize them for what they were until it was too late. Professor Stanislaus Scherzel was buried in Mountain View Cemetery in Prescott, which had opened about a year earlier. His grave was unmarked, very typical for suicides of the day. Such an event was considered shameful for the surviving family, while unceremoniously dumping the deceased into an unmarked grave, without even so much as a funeral, was considered normal. In those days, most churches and clergymen would not even officiate for a funeral of a suicide.

In 2005, ninety-three years after Scherzel's death, a small group of Prescott historians, including Elisabeth Ruffner, Nancy Burgess and myself, got together and obtained a tombstone for Professor Scherzel's grave (which was located on the cemetery map) in honor of his contribution to the historic Elks Opera House. A small ceremony was held, posthumously honoring him for having been part of the history of a theater that was, and still is, near and dear to our hearts.

THE OLD-FASHIONED GIRL

Lalie Brooks was on the vaudeville circuit nationwide with a comic wardrobe-changing routine set to music when she was booked to perform at the Elks Opera House in Prescott from February 24 to 27, 1914. Billed as "the Old-Fashioned Girl," she purported to display fashions from 1820 to 1920 (which was actually six years in the future). Miss Brooks, in her act, demonstrated a harem skirt, a Salome costume, a nineteenth-century hoop skirt and apparently a giant fig leaf (à la Eve) that covered her whole body (hardly a nineteenth-century fashion). This was 1914, so it is a certainty that all of her outfits were far more modest than anything you see on any city street in the present day.

Still, on Lalie Brooks's opening night, there were complaints from several audience members that the act was indecent and obscene. It is not known who the complainers were, but it is likely they were just a group of old biddies, the likes of which small towns of the era were notorious for. The next morning, the offended audience members marched over to the office of Prescott mayor William H. Timerhoff and demanded that he close down the show. In those days, towns and cities had the power to ban any type of entertainment within the city limits that they deemed offensive.

We will never know if Mayor Timerhoff was genuinely concerned by the allegation or if he simply knew that it was not politically healthy to ignore a group of old biddies in a small town. But he dropped what he was doing, rushed over to the Elks and demanded that Elks manager William Mays show him Miss Brooks's costumes, which were hanging in the dressing rooms. After not finding anything unseemly, he went back to his office and, to further placate the biddies, appointed a committee to attend the show that night to determine if it was indeed immoral. Manager Mays, frustrated by the incident, invited the Prescott City Council to attend as well.

By showtime on February 25, the *Journal Miner* had gotten wind of what was going on and sent a reporter to the Elks to try and interview the mayor's committee. After the show, the reporter collared police judge John H. Robinson and Prescott city councilman Harry Heap, both of whom denied seeing anything immoral in Lalie Brooks's show. The other committee members (there were at least two others) made a fast exit, undoubtedly embarrassed by the whole fracas.

The next morning, Mayor Timerhoff, the city council and the committee members met and proclaimed that Lalie Brooks could finish her run at the Elks.

FUNERAL MARCH OF THE KU KLUX KLAN

One of the most enduring stories of old Prescott is the brief history of the Ku Klux Klan in the area. The famed—or, rather, infamous—white supremacist group had existed in various forms throughout America since Southern Reconstruction following the Civil War. By the 1920s, the Klan was the subject of public debate, with state legislatures and other authorities conducting investigations into killings, vandalism and general terror tactics attributed to the Klan.

The first sign that the Ku Klux Klan had arrived in Prescott came on the night of October 23, 1922, when a huge cross was set ablaze on one of the hills overlooking the Government Canyon area. It was large enough to be visible to almost all of Prescott. Prescott Klan No. 14 was born, but it did not exert much influence in town in those days. The African American population was fairly small, so the Klan resorted to circulating pamphlets extolling its virtues and complaining about what it perceived as laxity on the part of Yavapai County officials in enforcing Prohibition laws. It singled out Yavapai County sheriff George C. Ruffner as the main target of this vendetta.

George C. Ruffner was sheriff from 1894 through 1898, in the days of train robberies, stagecoaches and horseback posses. He was the sheriff who hanged outlaw Fleming Parker in "The Parker Story." Now, in his old age, he decided he wanted his old job back and was elected sheriff once again in 1922, in the time of automobiles and Prohibition-era bootleggers. As sheriff in the modern era, it is known that Ruffner did not support Prohibition

Yavapai County sheriff George C. Ruffner stands front and center in a group photo with his deputies in front of the courthouse in Prescott in the 1920s. Ruffner had been sheriff in the 1890s in the days of horseback posses and train robberies and returned to the office in the 1920s in the days of automobiles and Prohibition bootleggers. He was targeted by the Ku Klux Klan for being purportedly lax on Prohibition enforcement. *Sharlot Hall Museum.*

and would often go as easy as he could on moonshiners. Prohibition is remembered with derision today, while bootleggers are remembered as simple men who sold illegal liquor primarily to feed their families during this period of tremendous economic depression. Sheriff Ruffner undoubtedly took all of this into account when forced by the law to go after them.

Prescott Klan No. 14 circulated a pamphlet around 1924, a copy of which is reposited today at Sharlot Hall Museum, that raged:

> *We receive many inquiries regarding law enforcement such as, why or by what authority does Sheriff Ruffner take upon himself the right to go out and destroy a bootlegger's still and turn the bootlegger loose? Was Sheriff Ruffner elected to office by the people to also act as Justice of the Peace, County attorney, Judge of the Court, and then tell the people he is saving the County money? Can Sheriff Ruffner prove to the people of Yavapai County that he has lived up to the oath of his office to the best of his ability?*

After more ranting and raving, the Klan pamphlet concluded:

All Klansmen of Prescott No. 14 take this occasion to recommend to the good people of Prescott that there is no better time than right now to clean up Prescott and Yavapai County [so] that we will be free of bootleggers and the vice conditions. To the bootlegger and dope peddler we have this to say: we are here to stay and Yavapai County is not large enough for all of us, so you may just as well make up your minds to leave or secure honest employment and be a real man or we shall do all in our power to see that you have free board and lodging with someone to watch you while you sleep.

There is no evidence that Sheriff Ruffner responded to this tirade. As sheriff, he certainly knew that Prescott Klan No. 14 was not making the inroads in Prescott that it had hoped to and was not gaining any real influence. By 1925, Prescott Klan No. 14 was frustrated by the lack of attention it was receiving, so it decided to do something flamboyant. One night, a group of hooded Klansmen marched into the First Baptist Church while services were going on, handed the pastor a large white envelope filled with cash and marched out again without speaking a word. Along with the money, the Klan had enclosed a note, which read:

We donate the sum of money enclosed herewith to be added to the building fund of your church. As you know, the principles of the nights of the Ku Klux Klan restrict their membership to those who accept the tenets of the true Christianity, which is essentially Protestant, and we hope you can find it consistent to accept this donation from men who serve and sacrifice to the right. To you and the good people of your church we extend all good wishes and our highest respect. Yours truly, Prescott Klan No. 14, Realm of Arizona, by Exalted Cyclops.

In May 1926, Joseph Holsom Drew, a seventy-eight-year-old worker in the incinerator plant at Fort Whipple (the military fort that had been stationed near Prescott for decades already), dropped dead while working. Drew was the son of the slave-owning third governor of Arkansas, Thomas Stevenson Drew, and was a well-liked and popular worker at the fort. However, in death, Prescott learned something about him it had not previously known: he had been a member of Prescott Klan No. 14. In those days, Klan members never divulged their identities or the identities of other members. The only exceptions were made in death, providing the Klan chose to do so, and it did in this case.

The Ku Klux Klan funeral march for Joseph Drew turns onto Gurley Street from Cortez Street in downtown Prescott in 1926. Note the Elks Opera House on the hill in the background. *Sharlot Hall Museum.*

The Ku Klux Klan, marching to Mountain View Cemetery to bury Joseph Drew, parades down Gurley Street. *Sharlot Hall Museum.*

The graveside service for Joseph Drew at Mountain View Cemetery, attended almost exclusively by robed and hooded Ku Klux Klansmen. *Sharlot Hall Museum.*

The tombstone of Joseph Drew as seen today in Mountain View Cemetery in Prescott. *David Schmittinger.*

Prescott Klan No. 14 decided to hold a full public Klan funeral for Joseph Drew. It even went so far as to buy ads in Prescott's two newspapers, the *Journal Miner* and the *Courier*, advising all members of the Klavern to attend. The memorial services for Drew were held at Lester Ruffner's funeral chapel, and then the funeral cortège, consisting of twenty-five hooded and robed Klansmen, left the service on foot and paraded down the streets of downtown Prescott in ritual formation, with the lead Klansman bearing an American flag. The procession was followed by the hearse and some non-Klan mourners. Local citizens massed along the streets, most of them attracted by curiosity, to witness Prescott's first (and, ultimately, only) Klan funeral procession.

The Klan marchers and the funeral procession headed for Mountain View Cemetery, nearly three miles away. There, Joseph Drew was buried in his Klan robes, and in Prescott history, he is the only one truly known to have been a member of Prescott Klan No. 14. The citizens of Prescott undoubtedly knew, or could guess, who other members were, but there is no surviving evidence.

Following this large public spectacle, Prescott Klan No. 14 disappeared from view after that. Deflated and perhaps financially hindered by Prescott's lack of interest in their cause, the Klavern just seems to have faded away. There are no records of any further Ku Klux Klan activity in Prescott after the funeral of Joseph Drew.

THE FORT WHIPPLE HANGING
OF DIXON SUJYNAMIE

The Yavapai-Apache Indian Reservation is located near Prescott, with part of it technically inside the city limits. But as late as 1935, it was still called the Fort Whipple Military Reservation, named for and overseen by the U.S. military fort that was located just outside Prescott. Fort Whipple is today the local Veterans Administration hospital.

On the evening of April 19, 1925, a sixty-three-year-old Prescott taxi driver named Arthur Cavell answered a call from the Fort Whipple Military Reservation (as it was then known) around 10:30 p.m. Upon arriving, the customer attacked Cavell and bludgeoned him to death with a fourteen-inch iron railroad spike. After dragging Cavell's body thirty feet off the road to hide it, the murderer stole the taxi cab and drove off. He left the murder weapon at the scene of the crime.

The next morning, local members of the Yavapai Indian tribe who were out hunting found the body and ran to the nearby home of the tribe's chief, Viola Jimulla, to report their discovery. The alarm was sounded, and authorities from Prescott and Yavapai County started investigating. By this time, Arthur Cavell's wife had also notified Yavapai County sheriff Edwin G. Weil that her husband was missing. (Cavell's body was shipped to Newton, Iowa, for burial.)

The first hours of the investigation did not go well, with Yavapai County deputies following many false leads. Sheriff's deputies quickly arrested four African Americans, based on a tip that Cavell's next taxi call following his trip to the reservation was to pick up a group of "negroes." They were later released. Further complicating the search was the belief that the crime had been committed by at least two perpetrators.

The case broke around midday with a tip from a gas station owner in Ash Fork, A.C. Keefe, who said an Indian driving a Ford sedan taxi (matching Cavell's vehicle) had stopped there for oil and gas. Keefe said the driver acted nervously and suspiciously and that, without being asked, the Indian had stated that he had just purchased the vehicle and was hoping to start his own taxi business in Winslow.

By late morning of April 20, Sheriff William Mahoney of Mohave County had arrested a Hualapai Indian wearing a bloodstained shirt in Kingman. The Indian was identified as twenty-eight-year-old George Dixon Sujynamie, and after severe questioning by Sheriff Mahoney, he broke down and confessed to the crime but insisted that a Navajo Indian named Frank Harper, who was with him, had struck the fatal blows. But in a statement issued to the *Prescott Courier*, Mahoney said, "The Indian is a bad man" and doubted he had any accomplices. However, based on the murderer's statement, Frank Harper was arrested but released in short order after providing a suitable alibi.

Shortly after Sujynamie's arrest, Cavell's blood-soaked car was found abandoned, along with some of his personal belongings that had been taken from the body, including a tire gauge, a knife and $3.50.

The next day, Yavapai County undersheriff Bert Savage and deputy county attorney Joseph C. Furst arrived in Kingman to take custody of George Dixon Sujynamie and return him to Yavapai County to stand trial. Under further questioning by Savage and Furst, Sujynamie gave up and made a full confession, admitting that he and he alone had murdered Arthur Cavell. He agreed to sign a written confession, which would be tantamount to a guilty plea, and therefore, there probably would not be a trial.

According to Sujynamie's confession, he was in love with a young Navajo woman, but because he was a Hualapai and not a Navajo, the woman's parents and other tribal members forbade their marriage. Deciding to get revenge, Sujynamie murdered Cavell solely to steal his car, so he could drive to Kingman and double back down the Big Sandy riverbed to where the girl lived. There, he said, he planned to murder her and the four tribal members who had told him they could not marry. After that, he said, he planned to commit suicide.

The girl in question was never publicly identified and was oddly not called as a witness in Sujynamie's trial. He would later say she was a Mohave Apache and not a Navajo.

The *Courier* reported that Sujynamie's shoes were his undoing. He had changed his shoes after the murder and put on a nice, good-looking pair.

He was picked up for questioning in Kingman for this reason, based on the presumption that an innocent Indian would not be wearing anything this good (today, this would be considered racial profiling) and also because a shoe store in the Mohave town of Hackberry had been robbed recently.

Sujynamie was arraigned in the Yavapai County Superior Court. He pleaded guilty, but his sentencing was delayed after it was brought up that the murder was committed on the Fort Whipple Military Reservation, which was federal land. This made the murder a federal case; therefore, it would need to be heard in the United States Federal Court in Prescott. Yavapai County attorney Edward S. Lyman told the *Courier* that he hoped the case would not be turned over to the feds because he wanted Sujynamie sentenced to death in "our own court."

After returning to the scene of the crime to look around, it was obvious Cavell had been murdered on the reservation. Sujynamie was turned over to United States commissioner J.F. Moreno, and he was brought before United States federal court judge Fred C. Jacobs. Here, George Dixon Sujynamie had a change of heart and refused to enter a guilty plea, as he said he would. He then asked for an attorney, and Judge Jacobs appointed Raymond B. Westervelt and Alfred B. Carr to represent the defendant. Assistant United States attorney George M. Wilson would handle the prosecution. It was clear that a trial was going to be held after all.

The trial of George Dixon Sujynamie for the murder of taxi driver Arthur Cavell commenced on July 7, 1925, in the United States District Court. Much time was spent trying to find impartial jurors, and interpreters were hired as some of the witnesses could not speak English. Although not recorded, the trial was probably held on the second floor of the Elks Opera House building in Prescott. The federal court had moved there in 1914 and likely stayed there until its new facility was built in the 1930s across Goodwin Street from the Yavapai County Courthouse.

After introducing all of the physical evidence in the murder, the prosecution's main witness was Lee Johnston, a Hualapai Indian in jail on a liquor charge, who shared the cell with Sujynamie upon his arrest. Johnston testified that he had known Sujynamie since he was a little boy and that the murderer had confessed to him as well. Johnston also testified that Sujynamie's parents and brother had visited him in jail and that he (Johnston) urged him to confess and get right with the Great Spirit. Johnston also testified that, in jail, Sujynamie had also shown erratic behavior. At one point, when a group of curious Hualapai girls stood outside the barred jail window hoping to get a glimpse of him, Sujynamie had looked out and started singing "My Wild Irish Rose."

The trial was interrupted at one point when Sujynamie jumped up and made a dash for the door, but he was quickly subdued and returned to his seat. At another point, he reportedly asked the deputies who were guarding him if they were good shots and said he was contemplating letting them find out. In the end, the murderer did not try to make another break for it. During a recess in proceedings, eleven members of the jury fêted fellow juryman W.F. Brannen for his seventy-fifth birthday and took him out to eat at the Owl restaurant.

The trial lasted only forty-eight hours, and Sujynamie's attorneys did not call any witnesses. The case went to the jury on July 9, 1925, and it returned with a verdict of guilty after only thirty-five minutes of deliberating. George Dixon Sujynamie was then sentenced to death by hanging by Judge Fred C. Jacobs. The next difficulty turned out to be where to hold the execution. The State of Arizona had moved all executions to the Arizona State Prison years earlier, but this was a federal case, which made a difference. United States marshal George Mauk, who was assigned to oversee the execution, asked Arizona governor George W.P. Hunt for permission to hold the hanging at the state prison, but Hunt had refused (the governor was actually an opponent of capital punishment, a highly unusual view for that era).

Marshal Mauk then met with Lawrence Ingraham, secretary for the Yavapai County Board of Supervisors, to discuss the possibility of having the execution held in Yavapai County. There had not been a legal hanging in Yavapai County since 1903, when Hilario Hidalgo and Francisco Renteria were hanged on the Courthouse Plaza in Prescott. Ingraham had reservations about this and told Mauk that the feds should consider hanging Sujynamie on federal land, as this had been a federal case. In the end, it was decided to hang George Dixon Sujynamie right on the Fort Whipple Military Reservation, at a location overlooking the scene of the crime where he had murdered Arthur Cavell. Judge Fred C. Jacobs set the date for October 10, 1925.

By mid-September, in the midst of rumors that Sujynamie would have his sentence commuted to life, U.S. marshal George Mauk pressed forward and hired Prescott carpenter Elmer Brennan to build the gallows. As usual, a twelve-foot stockade was to be built around the scaffold. Only invited guests could attend. A representative from the Washington-based Indian Rights Society, S.M. Crosius, arrived in Prescott to investigate the prospects of getting Sujynamie a commutation.

In some ways, times had changed since earlier-day hangings. Marshal Mauk had requested that the gallows be constructed with three electric pedal switches, which three of his deputies would push simultaneously. Two switches would be dummies, with one "live" one, and it would not be known which deputy pushed the fatal switch. This was a variation on the traditional executions by firing squad, where there were several shooters but only one with live ammunition and no one would know who fired the fatal shot.

On October 6, 1925, George Dixon Sujynamie asked for visits by Dr. Charles F. York, pastor of the First Methodist Church in Prescott. The doomed man was clearly starting to think about the hereafter and possibly making a "deathbed conversion." Marshal Mauk hired several Prescott residents as deputies to guard the scaffold day and night so no vandalism could occur. This prompted rumors in Prescott that the Hualapai tribe had informed Mauk that they would restart the Indian Wars and attack Fort Whipple if their brother was hanged.

The Indian Rights Society had petitioned U.S. president Calvin Coolidge for a commutation of Sujynamie's death sentence, but the chief executive refused to get involved. U.S. government physicians asked Mauk that Sujynamie's body be turned over to them for study, but Mauk refused, stating that it would be repatriated to his tribe. Meanwhile, the doomed Hualapai's last requests were that Dr. York, his minister, attend the hanging and that he be given a clean shirt to wear when he died, though he later asked for a full suit. He also requested that he be supplied with whiskey to give him courage, as he did not want to break down on the scaffold and shame his tribe.

Sujynamie, in his last days, also wrote a letter to the *Prescott Courier* newspaper, in which he blamed his crimes on the Mohave Apaches because they would not let him marry the girl he loved. The *Courier* printed it in full on October 8, 1925:

> *I wish to correct your statement on the issue of your paper of October 7 regarding my cast* [sic], *in which you said that I was going to the Big Sandy to get a Navajo girl.*
>
> *I presume you meant the girl whom the others was the cause of my trouble, she is a member of the Mohave Apache tribe of Indians and not a Navajo Indian.*
>
> *The others I refer to are also Mohave Apaches males and females and are living at the Indian camp near Prescott.*
>
> *Those males and females advised the girl not to marry me because I belong to the Wallapai tribe of Indians and because my grandfather was*

an Indian scout for the United States troops of long years ago and helped the troops to fight the Apache Indians at that time. For this reason they were prejudiced against me and their actions toward me regarding the girl whom I wanted to be my lawful wife aroused my anger and hatred against them to such an extent as to cause me to seek revenge of them. That is why I drove the car to Kingman, intending to go to the Big Sandy where I could secure a rifle, then come back to Prescott, kill my Apache Indian enemies and then kill myself.

I am heartily sorry that I killed Mr. Cavell and also sorry for his poor wife. I blame those Apache Indians for all my trouble for if it was not for their actions toward me, there would not be any murder committed by me and I would not be going to the scaffold there to be hanged on Saturday, October the 10th, so you can believe me that this is the whole truth and my God knows it is.

You have my permission to publish this letter in the column of your paper in your next issue of the same. I remain, yours very truly, George Dixon Sujynamie.

In lore of the old Southwest, which was becoming very popular in dime novels and silent movies, stories of playing cards being used as invitations to hangings were starting to appear. Although it probably had never really happened in the Old West, U.S. marshal George Mauk thought that was a pretty funny idea and decided to actually do it. To the fifty-two men invited to witness the hanging, Mauk sent out playing cards from a particular deck he owned, and these witnesses were to present the cards at the door. He also sent out a fake fifty-third card to a prospective witness who would then be denied admittance—apparently, Mauk thought that would be a good joke.

Among the invitees were all of the sheriffs and deputies from Yavapai and Mohave Counties. U.S. deputy marshal Robert Born and William A. Light, the superintendent of the Indian School at Truxton Canyon, near Valentine, Arizona (in Mohave County), finished the arrangements for Sujynamie's body to be sent to his father, Jack Sujynamie, and his tribe. It is unclear, but this school today may be the boarded-up Indian School ruin along Route 66 near Valentine.

On Sujynamie's final full day, Deputy Marshal Born delivered Sujynamie's requested new suit to him, and he received a haircut. He requested a chicken dinner with mashed potatoes and salad for his last meal. He spent his remaining hours writing letters to family and friends. He vowed to not break down and would die like a man so as not to bring shame to the Hualapai tribe.

Convicted murderer George Dixon Sujynamie is seen here with U.S. marshal George Mauk while being led to the scaffold at Fort Whipple, just minutes before he was hanged. He is holding a bouquet of flowers that was presented to him by the wife of his jailer. *U.S. Marshals Service.*

On October 10, 1925, Sujynamie spent the morning praying with Dr. York and leading the other prisoners in the singing of hymns. He was very talkative, and when escorted to the procession to take him to the gallows, several pictures of him were taken. He requested that Marshal Mauk make copies available to his friends. At about 11:35 a.m., the U.S. authorities, led by Marshal George Mauk, escorted George Dixon Sujynamie to the stockade overlooking the scene where he committed his horrible crime. He was not dressed in the new suit he had requested. He had either changed his mind or it was taken away from him for reasons unknown. He was simply dressed in a light shirt and blue pants. He ascended the gallows without hesitation, carrying a bouquet of flowers given to him by the wife of Alec M. Moore, the jailer at Fort Whipple.

Asked if he had any last words, he read aloud from two very lengthy written statements he had brought with him, delaying the execution somewhat. He read boldly, and the *Courier* reported he showed absolutely no fear of death. He asked that one of his statements, along with the bouquet of flowers, be buried with him and that his friend Smiling Bill Corthay be allowed to publish his life story, which he had written in jail (as far as I know, Sujynamie's manuscript has never been published and probably no longer exists). Finally, he asked to shake hands and say goodbye to several friends he spotted in the audience.

At 11:59 a.m., the black hood was pulled over Sujynamie's head and the three traps were sprung, sending him to his death.

Right: This is the platform for the gallows on which George Dixon Sujynamie was hanged. It is now owned by Sharlot Hall Museum in Prescott and was put on display as part of a law and order exhibit in 2015. *Sharlot Hall Museum.*

Below: This is the official death certificate for George Dixon Sujynamie, with his Hualapai name badly misspelled. His burial place is unknown, at least to nonmembers of the tribe, but is undoubtedly somewhere on the Hualapai Reservation. *Arizona Department of Vital Records.*

After the execution, the body of George Dixon Sujynamie was sent back home to the Hualapai tribe in Mohave County, where he was buried by them at an unknown location. Dr. Light, the superintendent of the Truxton Canyon Indian School, told the *Courier* that the Hualapai tribe was law abiding and horrified by Sujynamie's crime and that there was no truth to the rumors that the tribe had threatened to attack Fort Whipple if Sujynamie was hanged.

George Dixon Sujynamie was the eleventh and final hanging that occurred in the Prescott area between 1875 and 1925.

There is an unfortunate postscript to this story. Decades later, in October 1972, an old-time Prescott resident named Bill Simon wrote an article on this case for *AFFWord*, a now-defunct publication that was issued by a group called the Arizona Friends of Folklore that operated out of Northern Arizona University in Flagstaff. Despite its name, it contended that the stories it printed were largely true.

Simon's article was crudely titled "The Time We Hung the Indian." He did not mention Sujynamie by name—perhaps he didn't even remember it. But Simon claimed to be one of the men who was deputized to stand guard at the scaffold to prevent vandalism, and perhaps he was. He identified the other hired man as Pearly Morris, a local cowboy (he was actually Perlie Morris, a deputy sheriff from Seligman).

Contrary to the original accounts of Sujynamie's hanging, Simon wrote in his article that the Hualapai Indians had not only made threats against Fort Whipple but also that they actually surrounded the fort and beat drums, made loud war chants, unleashed stampeding horses and lit fires in the surrounding hills as warnings that the white man had better not hang their brother. Simon also claimed that on the day of the hanging, Fort Whipple had armed men riding around the borders to keep the Indians from attacking while the execution took place.

Since Simon claimed to have been there, it is easy to put stock in his account, and many have. But since it contradicts all of the primary accounts of the hanging from 1925, I do find myself wondering if Bill Simon was simply one of those old-time tall tale spinners, the kind who embellish stories in order to be entertaining. Such people have always been with us. Unfortunately, Simon's account has been taken seriously and repeated quite often in recent years, continuing to feed prejudices that still exist against Native Americans.

In his article, Bill Simon also claimed that, to kill time, he and Perlie Morris used rocks to test the three pedal switches to see which one was the live one and that they determined it was the middle switch. He further stated that a superstitious local resident named Roland Moser (his name was actually Roland Mosher) refused to be hired as one of the three deputies to push the switches, based on an old belief that the man who pulled the live switch would be dead within six weeks. In the end, Simon says, a man named Bill Stitch (supposedly a brother-in-law of famed Prescott rodeo cowman Doc Pardee) ended up being the deputy on the middle switch, and wouldn't you know it, Simon concludes, Stitch caught pneumonia and died within six weeks of the execution.

There was a Prescott resident at this time named Bill Stich. If this was the man Bill Simon was referring to, and it probably was, Stich actually died seven years later in 1932. But...never let the facts get in the way of a good story, right?

THE HATCHET MEN OF THE HOP SING TONG

It is very well known that Northern Arizona, including Prescott, had a very large population of Chinese residents in the late nineteenth and early twentieth centuries. However, Prescott's Chinatown (located on Granite Street) had completely disappeared by the 1940s, leaving behind only legends and folklore. As with the Mexican community, there was very little documentation of the Chinese when they were here, and any primary news accounts of them were largely unflattering.

Today, serious Prescott historians are bedeviled by folklore that the Chinese residents of old somehow constructed an elaborate tunnel system under downtown Prescott where they trafficked to and fro for God knows what reason. This folklore is pervasive, and many local historians are often accused of coverups when they deny that "Chinese tunnels" exist in Prescott. Never mind that the legend's believers cannot explain how Chinese peasants could have constructed such an elaborate and architecturally solid underground system without attracting any attention.

Many Chinese communities in America were also beset by tong activity. Chinese tongs were believed to be secret societies and/or gangs of Asians who were extremely powerful and were believed, by both Chinese and non-Chinese alike, to be virtually invincible, involved with organized criminal activity in the Asian neighborhoods. Even today, historians disagree about the reach and scope of the tongs. Tongs were considered to be very deadly, and they were often the subject of dime novels and old movies with anti-Chinese viewpoints in the early twentieth century.

As with all gangs, violence often erupted between rival tongs, who often sent out "hatchet men" assassins to dispatch their enemies. While such violence broke out in cities like San Francisco with heavy Chinese populations, it was not widely believed that the tongs reached into Arizona until October 20, 1926. On that fateful day, Tom King, a Chinese restaurateur of long residence in Kingman, was peeling potatoes in his American Kitchen restaurant when five other Asian men burst through the door with guns and opened fire, killing King instantly.

The official death certificate for Chinese Kingman restaurateur Tom King, whose Chinese name was apparently Gen Quen Yeck. He was murdered in a tong war between rival Chinese gangs. *Arizona Department of Vital Records.*

Mohave County authorities hit the trail of the murderers and caught up with them near the California state line. The five men were identified as B.W.L. Sam, Shew Chin, Jew Har, Gee King Long and Wong Lung. All five were further identified as hatchet men for the Bing Kong Tong. The dead man, Tom King, was revealed to have been a longstanding member of the Hop Sing Tong. Both tongs had been warring in America's larger cities for years, and now the violence had spread off the beaten path to Arizona. The Hop Sing Tong was regarded as one of the most powerful in America.

Alarmed by the outbreak of tong activity in Mohave County, Sheriff William Mahoney ordered a general "shakedown" of all Chinese residents, confiscating guns and ordering several of them to leave town (these were the days when lawmen could legally do things like this). Mahoney also asked Yavapai County to take the five tong killers to jail in Prescott, ostensibly as a safeguard against attempts on their lives by other hatchet men. The five were lodged in the Prescott jail shortly after that.

In December 1926, the tong killers went on trial in Prescott. Marring the proceedings was the sudden and mysterious disappearance of Don On, a restaurant customer who had been the only eyewitness to Tom King's murder. He was never found, dead or alive. Also raising apprehension in

Kingman was the arrival of three other tong members, ostensibly to go down to Prescott to witness the trial. Sheriff Mahoney placed them under arrest, even though they had caused no disturbance.

Despite these setbacks, the jury found the five tong hatchet men guilty of first-degree murder, and they were sentenced to hang at the Arizona State Prison in Florence. Their lawyers, probably paid for by the Bing Kong Tong, immediately appealed to the Arizona State Supreme Court. This delayed the executions for some time. The possibility of a successful appeal alarmed the Hop Sing Tong, which dispatched its top attorney, J.N. Young, to Arizona from Chicago. Arriving in Prescott on March 22, 1927, attorney Young immediately employed several prominent local attorneys (including Mohave County Superior Court judge E. Elmo Bollinger, Yavapai County attorney W.E. Paterson and assistant Yavapai County attorney John J. Sweeney) to represent the Hop Sing Tong during the appeals process. Attorney Young told the *Prescott Courier* that the Hop Sing Tong had over $1 million to spend to ensure that the killers' appeals would not be successful. Young also told

Above and opposite: These are the four official death certificates for Jew Har, Shew Chin, B.W.L. Sam and Gee King Long, the tong hatchet men who were executed in a quadruple hanging at the Arizona State Prison in Florence. *Arizona Department of Vital Records.*

the *Courier* that there were twenty Chinese businessmen in Prescott who were members of the Hop Sing Tong, a revelation that surely caused discomfort among Prescott's white residents.

The Arizona State Supreme Court upheld the death sentences of the five tong killers, but their execution was postponed again when Frank Craig, another witness at the trial, recanted his testimony and claimed that he had been bribed to testify as he did by attorney J.N. Young. After much legal wrangling and debating among the courts and the State Board of Pardons and Paroles, the execution date was set again, this time for June 23, 1928. At the last minute, Wong Lung's death sentence was commuted to life in prison because of his age; the tong hatchet man was only seventeen years old.

On June 23, 1928, the four assassins—B.W.L. Sam, Shew Chin, Jew Har and Gee King Long—were hanged at the Arizona State Prison in Florence, one right after the other. A legal quadruple hanging was rare even in those days, and in retrospect, it is surprising the tong murder case has been largely forgotten. Perhaps this is due to latter-day racial sensitivities and the fact that the story still has a chill to it, despite the passing of almost ninety years.

Do Chinese tongs still exist? Historians of Chinese culture are in debate about this. Some believe they died out due to modernizing of times, while others suspect they still exist but that they keep a much lower profile than they once did.

I'm Getting Tired
of Cowography

B y the 1920s and '30s, rodeos had become very popular nationwide and had advanced from mere feats of horsemanship, calf roping and bull riding to include halftime entertainment shows. During this period, one of the most popular of the entertainers and "singing cowboys" on the rodeo circuit was a man who went by the name of Powder River Jack Lee and his wife, Kitty. Despite their prominence, they are mostly forgotten today and are seldom talked about, even by rodeo historians. There is a reason for this.

Very little is known of the background of Jack H. Lee, except that his real name was Jackson Martin. He claimed to have been born and raised on a Montana ranch, breaking horses and riding on cattle drives from the time he could walk. At his rodeo appearances, he would regale the audiences with a story of how he and his wife, Kitty, had been childhood sweethearts in Montana, were separated by circumstances and then, by sheer happenstance, met again when they were adults at a chuck wagon on a cattle drive. Lee told the story so flamboyantly that listeners puddled up by the time it was over.

For her part, Kitty Lee (always introduced by her husband as "Pretty Kitty Lee") claimed to be a direct descendent of Andrew Jackson on her father's side and that she had once toured in Buffalo Bill's famous Wild West show—a claim that cannot be verified.

The very few documented facts about the Lees contradict their stories. Kitty Lee's death certificate, now public record, lists her birthplace as Beardstown, Illinois, not Montana. Furthermore, there is a record showing that Jack and

Kitty Lee played the Elks Opera House in Prescott on March 4–6, 1916, as a Hawaiian musical act. Surely no real cowman would have done that.

But in the 1920s nostalgia for the nineteenth-century Southwest was growing, with silent movies and dime novels glamorizing the era. People were hungry for cowboys, and during this time, many unsuccessful singers and entertainers, who had failed in other genres, started putting on cowboy hats and fraudulently passing themselves off as real cowmen. Some did find success in this, and Jack Lee, who adopted the moniker of "Powder River" when he changed his image, was one of them. Kitty Lee learned a few simple trick-riding skills, and soon both of them hit the rodeo circuit.

At rodeo halftime shows and state fair engagements, the Lees sang cowboy songs, recited cowboy poetry and told fanciful stories, many of which Lee claimed to have written himself. They were a hit and soon were touring rodeos nationwide and hobnobbing with important people like Will Rogers, Tom Mix, William S. Hart and famed cowboy artist Charles M. Russell. Jack and Kitty were even invited to the White House in 1937 to serenade the president's son and secretary, James Roosevelt, on his birthday.

Powder River Jack Lee started publishing books containing the song lyrics, prose, poems and stories that were allegedly his own compositions. He recorded his songs on phonograph records as well. He and Kitty even returned to the Elks Opera House in Prescott with their new cowboy image on March 27–29, 1929. One has to wonder if anyone in attendance remembered them from their "Hawaiian" appearance there in 1916. Certainly they trusted no one would.

Surprisingly, Powder River Jack Lee is forgotten today by historians, perhaps intentionally so. Perhaps this is because historians are virtually unanimous in the opinion that Lee plagiarized, or stole, much of his material. The most notable case was his phonograph recording of a song called "Tying Knots in the Devil's Tail" (which he also performed at his stage shows), an opus about two drunken cowboys who encounter the devil on a road, tie him up and brand him like a cow. Jack Lee took authorship credit in his songbooks and on the record labels, but Arizona residents quickly realized that the song was a slightly revamped version of "Sierry Petes," a famous poem written by Prescott's legendary pioneer Gail Gardner. Lee had altered a few things. In Gardner's original version, the two cowboys were named Buster Jig and Sandy Bob, wherein Lee changed their names to Buster Giggs and Sagebrush Sam. Lee changed other parts of the lyrics. In place of Gardner's stanza, "I'm sick of the smell of burnin' hair," Lee audaciously put "I'm getting tired of cowography."

Gail Gardner and the cowmen of Prescott were outraged by the theft. Stealing a cowman's song was almost as bad as stealing his horse. There is an enduring, but unverified, Prescott rodeo legend that Gardner and some other cowmen collared Jack Lee at a Whiskey Row saloon one night in downtown Prescott, tarred and feathered him and ran him out of town. If true, it did not faze him, as he continued to insist that he wrote "Tying Knots in the Devil's Tail" until his death.

All of this leaves a question that still lingers. If Powder River Jack Lee stole this song, how much more did he steal from other unknown authors and pass off as his own—authors who did not have Gardner's ability to fight back? There are reports that, at his stage shows, Lee

Prescott pioneer cowman Gail Gardner is seen here in the early 1900s. He also wrote cowboy poetry, including the famous "Sierry Petes," which was plagiarized by Powder River Jack Lee. *Sharlot Hall Museum.*

claimed to be the original author of the legendary song "Red River Valley," a claim that cannot possibly be true.

Lee's reputation as a musical thief has dogged him long after his death. He is one of the few successful singers of the era whose recordings have not been reissued on CD. His recording of "Tying Knots in the Devil's Tail" has appeared on a small handful of anthology albums of old cowboy music, but most of his recordings have not seen the light of day in over seventy years.

In some ways, it is really too bad that Powder River Jack Lee was such a fraud. He actually did have talent, his books are enjoyable lightweight reads, his recordings (if you can find them) have a jaunty air about them that makes them very entertaining and he made people happy. Unfortunately, it

Powder River Jack and Kitty Lee serenade James Roosevelt (the president's son and secretary) at the White House on the occasion of the younger Roosevelt's birthday. They performed their stolen version of "Tying Knots in the Devil's Tail." *Library of Congress.*

cannot be denied that he achieved a lot of this through unscrupulous means; therefore, historians prefer not to discuss him.

Powder River Jack Lee was killed in a car accident in Chandler, Arizona, in 1946. Soon after that, Kitty Lee entered the Arizona Pioneer Home (the state-owned nursing home in Prescott), blind and partially deaf, until her own death in 1955 at the age of eighty-nine. Both are interred at the City of Mesa Cemetery.

AFTERWORD

Prescott, Arizona, remains rich in history and is one of the key towns in Arizona history overall. In bygone eras, significant political and cultural events and history occurred here, from ranching to mining to the more unfortunate events we have seen in these pages.

In spite of that, Prescott remains a bustling centerpiece of Arizona and regularly appears on lists of the best places to retire in America. Its history is well preserved by a number of museums, such as Sharlot Hall Museum, the Smoki Museum, the Phippen Museum and others. A number of highly regarded individual historians are also active in preservation of our past.

I invite you to visit Prescott or, if you already live here, to come and explore our historical heritage, including our "wicked" side of history!

BIBLIOGRAPHY

THE U.S. GOVERNMENT CREATES ARIZONA

Gressinger, A.W. *Charles D. Poston—Sunland Seer*. Globe, AZ: D.S. King, 1961.

Henson, Pauline. *Founding a Wilderness Capital*. Flagstaff, AZ: Northland Press, 1965.

Poston, Charles Debrille. *Building a State in Apache-Land*. Tempe, AZ: Aztec Press, Inc., 1963.

Poston, Lawrence, III. "Poston Vs. Goodwin." *Arizona and the West* 3, no. 4 (Winter 1961).

THE TERRITORY OF ARIZONA CREATES PRESCOTT

Munderloh, Terry. "Days Past; The Traveling Territorial Capital." www.sharlot.org/archives/dayspast.

PRESCOTT'S FIRST MURDERED WOMAN

Weekly Arizona Miner, various issues, 1870.

THE FIRST HANGING—FACT AND FOLKLORE

Barney, James M., and Charles M. Clark. "The Story of the First Legal Hanging in Prescott, Yavapai County." *Sheriff Magazine*, March 1956.
Weekly Arizona Miner, various issues, 1875.

SHOOTOUT WITH VIRGIL EARP

Chaput, Donald. *Virgil Earp—Western Peace Officer*. Norman: University of Oklahoma Press, 1996.
Weekly Arizona Miner, various issues, 1875.

THE SKELETON ON THE COURTHOUSE PLAZA

Weekly Arizona Miner, various issues, 1876–82.

THE BLOODIEST DAY IN COURT

Sharlot Hall Museum. Vertical File Folder: Charles W. Beach.

THE MURDER OF OLD TEX

Weekly Arizona Miner, various issues, 1881.

GOOD-BYE, OLD BOY

Weekly Arizona Miner, various issues, 1881–82.

BIBLIOGRAPHY

THE DILDA CASE

Sharlot Hall Museum. Vertical File Folder: Dilda, Dennis W.
Weekly Arizona Miner, various issues, 1885–86.

HORRIBLE THEY WERE

Sharlot Hall Museum. Vertical File Folder: The Horribles.

ANNIE'S FALLEN ANGELS

Anderson, Parker. "Days Past; in the Matter of Annie Hamilton." www.
sharlot.org/library-archives/days-past.

THE CLEVENGER KILLINGS

Anderson, Parker. "Days Past; True Crime: Frank Wilson and the Clevenger
Murders." www.sharlot.org/library-archives/days-past.
Weekly Arizona Miner, various issues, 1887.

I GUESS I WILL GO ASLEEP NOW

Anderson, Parker. "Days Past; a Life Cut Short: The 1887 Murder of Reyes
Baca." www.sharlot.org/library-archives/days-past.
Weekly Arizona Miner, various issues, 1887.

THE MAN WHO COULD NOT STAY OUT OF TROUBLE

Anderson, Parker. "Story of a Hanged Man." Unpublished manuscript, n.d.
Weekly Arizona Miner, various issues, 1894.

THE BLUE DICK

Weekly Arizona Journal Miner, various issues, 1895.
Yavapai County Superior Court Records. Arizona State Library and Archives.

THE LARK PIERCE MANHUNT

Prescott Courier, various issues, 1895.
Weekly Arizona Journal Miner, various issues, 1888 and 1895.

MURDER AT THE KEYSTONE

Weekly Arizona Journal Miner, various issues, 1895.

THE PARKER STORY

Anderson, Parker. "Story of a Hanged Man." Unpublished manuscript, n.d.
Weekly Arizona Journal Miner, various issues, 1897–98.

George C. Ruffner's Bad Week

Anderson, Parker. "Days Past; Local Doctor, John Bryan McNally, Shot by Deranged Prospector, 1898." www.sharlot.org/library-archives/days-past.

Weekly Arizona Journal Miner, various issues, 1898.

The Goddard Station Murders

Anderson, Parker. "Days Past; Jacinto Cota Prosecuted for Perjury, 1903." www.sharlot.org/library-archives/days-past.

———. "Days Past; Racial Inequality Evident in 1903 Murder and Hanging in Yavapai County." www.sharlot.org/library-archives/days-past.

Arizona Journal Miner, various issues, 1903.

A Long Life of Trouble

Prescott Journal Miner, various issues, 1908–10.

Ombre Muerte on Thumb Butte

Anderson, Parker. "Days Past; Leaving a Dead Man on Thumb Butte Seemed Like a Good Idea." www.sharlot.org/library-archives/days-past.

Prescott Journal Miner, various issues, 1911.

Yavapai County Coroner Inquests. Arizona State Library and Archives.

Will Morfia from the Air in a Small Jar

Anderson, Parker. "Days Past; Three Unusual Deaths from the Summer of 1912." www.sharlot.org/library-archives/days-past.

Prescott Journal Miner, various issues, 1912.

Yavapai County Coroner Inquests. Arizona State Library and Archives.

ELKS OPERA HOUSE

Anderson, Parker. "The Elk That Roared: Memories of a Frontier Opera House." Unpublished manuscript, n.d.
Yavapai County Coroner Inquests. Arizona State Library and Archives.

FUNERAL MARCH OF THE KU KLUX KLAN

Anderson, Parker. "Days Past; a Brief History of the Ku Klux Klan in Prescott." www.sharlot.org/library-archives/days-past.
Prescott Courier, various issues, 1926.
Prescott Journal Miner, various issues, 1926.
Sharlot Hall Museum. Vertical File Folder—Organizations—Ku Klux Klan.

THE FORT WHIPPLE HANGING OF DIXON SUJYNAMIE

Prescott Courier, various issues, 1925.
Prescott Journal Miner, various issues, 1925.
Simon, Bill. "The Time We Hung the Indian." *AFFWord*, October 1972.

THE HATCHET MEN OF THE HOP SING TONG

Anderson, Parker. "Days Past; a Story of Chinese Gangs in Northern Arizona." www.sharlot.org/library-archives/days-past.
Prescott Courier, various issues, 1926–28.

I'M GETTING TIRED OF COWOGRAPHY

Anderson, Parker. "The Saga of 'Powder River' Jack and Kitty Lee." www.sharlot.org/library-archives/days-past.

About the Author

Parker Anderson is an Arizona native and a recognized historian in Prescott. He is the author of the books *Elks Opera House*, *Cemeteries of Yavapai County* and *Grand Canyon Pioneer Cemetery*. He has written articles for "Days Past," the weekly history column in the *Prescott Courier* newspaper, and authored a number of Arizona history plays for Blue Rose Theater. He resides in Prescott.